SOUNDS LiKE FUN

Family Place Collection
Funded by the Carpenter Grant

Riverside Public Library

SOUNDS LiKE FUN

Activities for Developing Phonological Awareness

REVISED EDITION

by

Cecile Cyrul Spector, Ph.D.

·P·A·U·L·H·
BROOKES
PUBLISHING Co ®

Baltimore • London • Sydney

Paul H. Brookes Publishing Co.
Post Office Box 10624
Baltimore, Maryland 21285-0624
USA

www.brookespublishing.com

Manufactured in the United States of America by
Versa Press, Inc., East Peoria, Illinois.

This book was previously published by Thinking Publications as
Sound Effects: Activities for Developing Phonological Awareness
(ISBN-10: 1-888222-37-9).

Library of Congress Cataloging-in-Publication Data

Spector, Cecile Cyrul
   Sounds like fun : activities for developing phonological awareness / by Cecile Cyrul
Spector. -- Rev. ed.
      p.   cm.
   Rev. ed. of: Sound Effects. Eau Claire, Wis : Thinking Publications, c1999.
   ISBN-13: 978-1-59857-048-9
   ISBN-10: 1-59857-048-X
   1. Children—Language.   2. English language—Phonetics.   3. Plays on words.   4.
Language arts (Primary)—Activity programs.   I. Spector, Cecile Cyrul, Sound effects.
II. Title.

LB1139.L3S664 2009
372.46'5—dc22   2009007996

British Library Cataloguing in Publication data are available from the British Library.

2013   2012   2011   2010   2009

10   9   8   7   6   5   4   3   2   1

CONTENTS

A pun is the lowest form of wit,
It does not tax the brain a bit;
One merely takes a word that's plain
And picks one out that sounds the same.
Perhaps some letter may be changed
Or others slightly disarranged,
This to the meaning gives a twist,
Which much delights the humorist.
A sample now may help to show
The way a good pun ought to go:
"It isn't the cough that carries you off,
It's the coffin they carry you off in."

–Unknown

PREFACE

The need for this book became clear to me during the collection and analysis of data for a research study. More than two hundred students, in grades three through six, took part in the study designed to assess understanding of humor based on phonological changes. Twelve of each type of humor item represented in *Sounds Like Fun (i.e.,* sound addition, substitution, and deletion) were used. The data gathered from students with normal achievement were separated from the data gathered from students with language-learning disorders (enrolled in the schools' speech-language intervention programs), and those with reading deficits (enrolled in the schools' remedial-reading programs). The number of students who had both language-learning disorders and reading deficits was striking. This latter group of students had the lowest number of correct responses. This finding may come as no surprise to speech-language pathologists working in school settings, or remedial-reading teachers. It became apparent to me that the phonological awareness skills needed to decipher humor based on phonological changes are essential for both language and reading development.

The next step was to see if students with language-learning and reading difficulties could be trained to develop the phonological awareness skills needed to respond appropriately to questions about the humor items. The answer was a resounding yes! After approximately eight weeks of having students work on phonological humor items, in the manner set forth in *Sounds Like Fun,* their responses greatly improved. Many of the students indicated that they found the humor items enjoyable, and several of them even offered similar humor items of their own.

Most intervention products on the market focus on the improvement of expressive phonology; that is, perceiving and articulating particular phonemes in words, or dealing with phonological processes such as syllable deletion, final consonant deletion, stopping, or cluster reduction. In the past, clinicians have focused on expressive phonology, with improved intelligibility as the goal (Hodson, 1994). However, research findings (e.g., Ball, 1997; Blachman, 1994) indicate that children with disordered phonology frequently lack metaphonological awareness skills, which allow them to analyze the sound system consciously (e.g., awareness of the phonological segments in words, and the ability to manipulate these segments).

Determining phonological changes in humor items is merely a vehicle for the development of phonological awareness skills. A deficiency in phonological awareness affects language comprehension, literacy development, and spelling acquisition, and, consequently, most academic subjects.

Phonological awareness skills develop as they relate to other language factors (i.e., morphology, syntax, semantics, and pragmatics). For example, to understand the type of sound changes found in *Sounds Like Fun,* Students must be able to see the connection between the phonological and semantic aspects of the target words in the humor items.

ACKNOWLEDGMENTS

This revised edition of *Sound Effects: Activities for Developing Phonological Awareness* (Thinking Publications, 1999), retitled *Sounds Like Fun: Activities for Developing Phonological Awareness, Revised Edition,* has been ably brought into its current form with the assistance of several very nice people at Brookes Publishing Co. Amy Kopperude, Production Designer, provided many constructive suggestions, the very readable format, and the delightful graphics seen throughout the pages of the book. I am grateful to Sarah Shepke for steering this book through the acquisitions process. Other individuals at Brookes Publishing who were involved with the *Sounds like Fun* project are Melanie Allred, Tara Cellinese, and Jen Lillis. I thank them for their help. My thanks also to the reviewers for their valuable insights, suggestions, and criticisms.

I also owe thanks to my husband, Mort, and my entire family for their unfailing encouragement and support of my writing efforts.

INTRODUCTION

Sounds Like Fun: Activities for Developing Phonological Awareness, Revised Edition provides facilitators with materials to help students in grades 3–12 develop their metaphonological skills, which are also referred to simply as phonological awareness skills. Metaphonological skills enable a student to reflect on and consciously manipulate phonological segments (Hodson, 1994). This resource uses phonological humor as a vehicle for developing metaphonological skills, as well as other metalinguistic skills.

The following groups of students may benefit from the activities in *Sounds Like Fun*:

- Those who present normal achievement but need to strengthen their metalinguistic, and particularly their metaphonological (i.e., phonological awareness), skills
- Those who have language-learning disabilities
- Those who have reading disabilities
- Those who are learning English as a second language (ESL)

Facilitators who might work with such students include speech-language pathologists, classroom teachers of students in grades 3–12, special education teachers, learning disabilities specialists, remedial reading specialists, teachers of students with a hearing impairment, and teachers of ESL.

Sounds Like Fun includes the following types of activities:

- *Warm-up Activities* to improve awareness of how phoneme changes affect the meaning of words. The activities are arranged according to the following tasks:
  - Take away a consonant sound (e.g., Take away a consonant sound to make the word *gray* a word that means "a beam of sunlight." (*ray*))
  - Change a consonant sound (e.g., Change a consonant sound to make the word *pleat* a word that means "icy rain." (*sleet*))
  - Change a vowel sound (e.g., Change a vowel sound to make the word *bag* a word that means "the opposite of little." (*big*))
  - Add a consonant sound (e.g., Add a consonant sound to make the word *it* a word that means "the stone in the center of a peach." (*pit*))

  Each *Warm-up Activity* is immediately followed by a review page. The purpose of the review page is to provide additional phonological awareness practice and to ensure that students have the necessary skills to manipulate sound changes in words.
- *Phonological Humor Activities* grouped into units according to the nature of the phoneme task (i.e., Take Away a Consonant Sound, Change a Consonant Sound, Change a Vowel Sound, Add a Consonant Sound). After each item are four questions that ask students to do the following:
  - Detect the word that has a sound change to make the joke or riddle funny.
  - Infer what the funny word was before the sound change was made.
  - Identify the context clues indicating why the funny word was used.
  - Explain why the funny word was used.

The *Phonological Humor Activities* in each unit are followed by a Review and Reflection task. The purpose of this task is to ensure that students comprehend the activities they have just completed and grasp their relevancy.

- *Challenge Activities*, including phonological humor items with a combination of sound changes (e.g., addition and substitution); these items inspire students to make full use of divergent-thinking skills
- *Additional Activities*, offering a variety of ways to explore multiple sound changes to the same word (e.g., Take Away a Sound, Then Two), followed by activities for knock-knock jokes, which contain phonological-based humor but lack the context of the jokes and riddles in Units 1–5

GOALS

The overall goal of *Sounds Like Fun* is to offer enjoyable activities that help students develop phonological awareness. More specifically, the intent of *Sounds Like Fun* is to

- Provide students with opportunities to focus on the constituent phonemes of words and to manipulate them with regard to their meaning
- Strengthen students' understanding of the difference between the graphemic and phonemic representation of words
- Improve students' comprehension and production of items that have sounds added, substituted, or deleted from target words
- Challenge students to apply phonological awareness skills to real-life contexts
- Enhance students' divergent-thinking skills, mental associations, and vocabulary
- Develop a greater awareness of the relationships among phonology, morphology, syntax, semantics, and pragmatics

PHONOLOGICAL AWARENESS AND META-SKILLS

Many skills are needed to manipulate and demonstrate understanding of the sound system of the English language, including the following:

- Grasping sound–symbol correspondence, direct or otherwise (e.g., /f/ = f in *fun*, but /f/ = *gh* in *laugh*)
- Segmenting and redefining a phonological string
- Analyzing and integrating syntactic information
- Interpreting contextual information
- Inferring meaning
- Perceiving and using paralinguistic cues (e.g., vocal intensity, stress, intonation)
- Evoking new and different meanings in words, phrases, and sentences
- Putting into words what is known implicitly

Children's ability to segment syllables into phonemes develops gradually between 6 and 10 years of age as they become more adept at attending to the phonemic aspects of words (Wallach & Miller, 1988). The ability to segment words into their constituent phonemes is the culminating skill of *phonological awareness*. Other skills include blending, rhyme recognition, sound manipulation, sound-to-word matching, and phoneme specification (Lewkowicz, as cited in Stackhouse, 1997). The review pages for *Warm-up Activities* in *Sounds Like Fun* are based on these six skill areas. The *Phonological*

Humor Activities and *Challenge Activities* help students develop metaphonological awareness, as they explain the phoneme changes that create jokes and riddles.

Using the materials in this book, facilitators can help students develop their ability to detect, infer, and explain phoneme level changes. In this way, morphophonemic and semantic skills are integrated and complex metaphonological skills are developed or improved. Pragmatic skills are also enhanced as students become familiar with the dynamics of joke telling and learn how to appropriately respond to humor created by sound changes.

DIFFICULTIES IN ACQUIRING PHONOLOGICAL AWARENESS

Some children need direct instruction to develop phoneme segmentation skills (van Kleeck, 1990). Many factors may account for difficulties in acquiring phonological awareness and in completing phoneme manipulation tasks. Among these factors are the following:

- There is not always a one-to-one correspondence between a sound and its alphabetic symbol. The same alphabetic symbol can represent more than one sound. For example, *c* may represent either /s/ (as in *city*) or /k/ (as in *cat*). Also, different alphabetic symbols can represent the same sound. For example, both *c* and *k* can represent /k/ (as in *cat* and *kite*). In addition, when certain alphabetic symbols are combined, they can represent a single sound. For example, in the word laugh, *l* represents /l/, but *au* represents /æ/ and *gh* represents /f/; thus there are five letters in *laugh* but only three sounds /l/ /æ/ /f/). (See the appendix for further examples of consonant and vowel sound–symbol correspondence.)

- The acoustic patterns of consonants are influenced by the vowels that surround them. The speaker starts to shape his or her mouth to form the medial vowel while still saying the initial consonant. For example, the /b/ in *boy* has a different acoustic pattern that the /b/ in *bat*.

- The consonant's position within the syllable can affect its acoustic pattern. For example, the /p/ in *pat* is aspirated; the /p/ in *top* is not.

- Morphophonemics and semantics further complicate the acquisition of phonological awareness. Words that are spelled differently and have different meanings can be pronounced the same way. For example, *to*, *too*, and *two* are all pronounced /tu/.

- Words that look the same can be pronounced differently depending on the context, such as the word *read*, when referring to the present or past tense.

- Children may be successful in segmenting syllables, but may fail to classify those segments according to the adult phonological system. For example, children may treat /tʃ/ and /tr/ as allophones and, therefore, would regard *chain* and *train* as alternate pronunciations of the same word. Such misconceptions would have an impact on the acquisition of an alphabetic reading strategy (Treiman, 1991).

- Coarticulation (i.e., an overlapping of sounds) often obscures phonemic units; consequently, it may not be possible to determine where one sound ends and the next sound begins (Liberman, Shankweiler, & Liberman, 1989).

- The ability to segment words into their constituent phonemes does not appear to occur as a natural consequence of learning spoken language. Learning to segment requires that attention be drawn specifically to the level of the phoneme (Adams, 1990; Gough, Juel, & Griffith, 1992).

· How sounds are perceived depends on characteristics such as the age, gender, and identity of the speaker, as well as the rate of speech (Bird, Bishop, & Freeman, 1995).

Phonological awareness skills do not develop in isolation. Communication behavior involves an interaction among phonology, morphology, syntax, semantics, and pragmatics. Development of each of these linguistic components affects the others. Researchers have pointed out the connection between phonological awareness and other aspects of language (Ball, 1997; Ball & Blachman, 1988; McGregor, 1994; Menyuk & Chesnick, 1997). McGregor, for example, found that using phonological information (e.g., initial sound and number of syllables in a target word) helped reduce semantic errors in word-finding tasks. This conclusion shows the link between semantic and phonological information in lexical storage and access.

There are many levels of phonological awareness (Rubba, 2004). Shallow and intermediate phonological awareness skills include awareness that sentences and phrases can be broken down into single words, some words share sounds or sound sequences, a word can be divided into its component syllables, and a syllable can be broken down into onsets and rimes (e.g., *slat* has the onset /sl/ and the rime /at/). Deep phonological awareness skills include awareness that a single sound (i.e., phoneme) in a word can be changed to create a new word, a word can be segmented into its constituent phonemes, the number of phonemes in a word can be counted and each phoneme identified, and phonemes within a word can be manipulated to create new words. These deep phonological awareness skills pertain to phonemes and, thus, are called *phonemic awareness skills.*

Given that the components of language are intertwined, a student with poor phonological awareness may have other language-learning difficulties. If this is the case, a considerable amount of support from the facilitator will be necessary if such a student is to develop the ability to phonologically manipulate the stimulus items in *Sounds Like Fun.* Students should be made aware of and encouraged to use all available morphological, syntactic, semantic, and pragmatic cues to comprehend the items.

METAPHONOLOGICAL AWARENESS, READING, AND SPELLING

Metaphonological awareness is achieved when students know about their ability to segment and manipulate the phonemes that comprise a word. Children who have developed metaphonological competence can use what they already know about manipulating phonemes to decipher unfamiliar words.

Several basic metaphonological skills are necessary to successfully complete the activities in *Sounds Like Fun.* For example, before students can segment a word into its constituent phonemes, they must be able to

· Hear the similarity of rhyming words
· Segment sentences into word units
· Segment multisyllabic words into syllables
· Identify the initial phoneme in a word
· Identify the final phoneme in a word

- Identify a targeted middle phoneme in a word
- Identify a targeted phoneme within a consonant blend

Although these skills are commonly acquired by the time a child is 5¹/2 or 6 years old, for some children it is necessary to strengthen (or develop) these skills (Blachman, 1991).

Children who lack the metaphonological skills needed for phonemic segmentation and manipulation tasks are likely to experience difficulty with reading and spelling (Bradley & Bryant, 1985; Clarke-Klein, 1994; Fischer, Shankweiler, & Liberman, 1985; Treiman, 1991). Menyuk and Chesnick (1997) concur that children who have difficulty in bringing phonological segments in words to awareness will have difficulty learning to read.

Approximately 30% of first graders do not have an understanding of the phonological structure of words (Adams, 1990; Robertson, 1993). Researchers such as Gillon (2002) and Hogan, Catts, and Little (2005) suggest that enhancing children's phonological awareness can significantly improve reading performance in children with reading difficulties. Gillon indicates that measuring phonological awareness at the phoneme level is a more powerful and accurate predictor of reading success than factors such as intelligence, vocabulary knowledge, or socioeconomic status. Browder (2008) found that phonemic awareness is a predictor of early reading success.

In their study of the relationship between phonological awareness and reading, Hogan et al. (2005) found a reciprocal relationship between phonological awareness and word reading. Kindergartners' phonological awareness predicted their second-grade word reading, and conversely, second graders' word reading predicted their fourth-grade phonological awareness.

Catts (1993) assessed reading achievement in terms of word recognition in first- and second-grade children who had been identified in kindergarten as having semantic-syntactic speech-language disorders. Catts found that deficits in phonological awareness are often closely associated with reading disabilities and concluded that programs to improve reading ability should be supplemented with activities to improve phonological awareness. Torgesen, Wagner, and Rashotte (1994) found that two particular phonological awareness skills—phonological analysis (i.e., breaking down words into their constituent phonemes) and phonological synthesis (i.e., blending phonemes into words)—are strongly related to reading proficiency.

Researchers have provided ample evidence of reciprocal influences between phonological awareness and both literacy acquisition and spelling (Adams, 1990; Ball, 1997; Ball & Blachman, 1991; Blachman, 1994; Fletcher, Shaywitz, Shank-weiler, Katz, Liberman, et al., 1994; Morais, 1991; Perfetti, 1991; Pressley & Rankin, 1994; Schuele & Boudreau, 2008; Torgesen et al., 1994; Wagner & Torgesen, 1987; Williams, 1986). The greater a child's awareness of the phonological structure of words prior to reading instruction, the greater that child's success in learning to read (Blachman, 1991; Ball & Blachman, 1991; Bradley & Bryant, 1985; Lundberg, Frost, & Petersen, 1988; Torgesen et al., 1994). Similarly, a child's awareness of phonemic segments is essential for spelling acquisition (Clarke-Klein, 1994).

Evidence also indicates that instruction in phonological awareness positively influences later reading and spelling performance (Ball & Blachman, 1988; Bradley & Bryant, 1991; Gillon & Dodd, 1995; Hurford, Johnston, Nepote, Hampton, Moore, et al., 1994; Lundberg et al., 1988; Pokorni, Worthington, & Jamison, 2004; Swanson, Hodson, &

Schommer-Aikins, 2005). Lundberg et al. (1988), for example, found that children who had received phonological awareness training had significantly higher levels of reading and spelling achievement over the 3-year span covered in their study than children who had not been trained.

Stothard Snowling, Bishop, Chipchase, and Kaplan (1998) noted that children who did not have phonological awareness training during intervention for speech impairment—and were subsequently discharged as their speech-production difficulties were resolved—were found to have reading difficulties at age 15. Perhaps, posited Stothard et al., speech and language intervention programs that include phonological awareness activities may prevent future literacy problems. In fact, Gillon (2002) found that

> Children with severe expressive phonological impairment and severe phonological awareness deficits responded quickly to an integrated phonological awareness intervention implemented by an SLP. Children who received that intervention showed significant gains in speech production, phonological awareness, reading, and spelling development. (p. 4)

Gillon stated that 11 months after intervention, most of the children were reading at or above the expected level for their age.

Results of studies by Ball and Blachman (1988) and Bradley and Bryant (1991) show that phonological awareness skills can be taught to nonreaders and that this training fosters success in reading and spelling. In fact, early problems with phonological awareness that persist into the high school and college years continue to interfere with reading performance (Apthorp, 1995; MacDonald & Cornwall, 1995).

Studies by Kitz and Tarver (1989) and Pennington, Van Orden, Smith, Green, and Haith (1990) have shown that adolescents and adults with reading disabilities continue to perform at lower levels than their peers on phonological awareness tasks. Snyder and Downey (1991) have suggested that older children with reading disabilities, because they lack adequate phonological awareness skills, may place greater reliance on context and higher level discourse processing skills for reading comprehension.

When teaching children to read, adults often need to focus on the nature of the language's sound–symbol correspondence. Phonics instruction in reading depends on a child's ability to understand that words can be segmented into phonemes. Children who learn phonological awareness and segmentation should participate in language comprehension activities as well; it is not an *either–or* situation (Ball, 1997). Children must be able to monitor meaning and recognize cues that supply information. The activities in *Sounds Like Fun* were developed to connect phonological awareness with the semantic aspects of language. Given that research shows a strong interrelationship among phonological awareness, reading, and spelling, the activities in this resource will likely provide a means for improving all three.

HUMOR BASED ON PHONEME CHANGES

In a study designed to examine metaphonological awareness (Spector, 1997), children as young as 8 years old were shown to be capable of grasping some of the humor based on phoneme level changes. The children in this study were significantly better at detecting the word that contained the sound change and inferring what that word could be than explaining the nature of the change. The ability to explain was found to improve significantly between the ages of 8 and 11 years.

Adolescents with language development disorders had a significantly poorer comprehension of phonological humor elements than did adolescents with typical language development in a study of adolescents' linguistic humor comprehension (Spector, 1990). The same held true for children between 8 and 11 years old with language development disorders when compared with their peers with typical language development (Spector, 1997).

Humor items for children are frequently based on the manipulation of phonological segments (e.g., those created using minimal pairs) (Green & Pepicello, 1978; Pepicello, 1980; Spector, 1990, 1997). The inability to express or understand the phonological elements that cause humor can create problems in coping with school, social, and vocational situations in which such humor is used (Donahue & Bryan, 1984; Nippold, 1988; Spector, 1990, 1992; Wiig, 1984).

In *Sounds Like Fun*, the Phonological Humor Activities are based on the addition, substitution, or deletion of a sound in a word. The Challenge Activities are based on a combination of any of these three. Humor items that have a sound added or a sound substituted appear to be easier for children to understand than humor items that have a sound deleted. Perhaps the items with a sound added are easier because they are visually salient; the correct response is already part of the word that is seen. Finding the word that was changed to make the joke or riddle funny requires merely the removal of the added sound. For example, the humor in "How do fireflies start a race?...Ready, set, glow!" is based on the addition of /l/ to a word in the familiar phrase "Ready, set, go!" Contextual support (i.e., *fireflies* and *race*) assists in the process of determining which sound to remove. Spector (1997) found that going from a consonant cluster to a single consonant (*glow—go*) appears to be simpler than going from a single consonant to a consonant cluster (*tooth—truth*).

For humor items that have a sound substituted, discerning whether distinctions between consonants or between vowels is easier is not clear. Perceiving differences between sounds, whether consonants or vowels, is probably determined by how similar two sounds are in their distinctive features. For example, the difference between /f/ and /θ/ is difficult to perceive because only one feature is different: the placement of the articulators (i.e., labiodental versus linguadental). It is easier to distinguish between /p/ and /g/ because several features are different: /p/, a voiceless, bilabial sound, is produced in the front of the mouth, whereas /g/, a voiced, velar sound, is produced in the back of the mouth. Similarly, it may be difficult to distinguish between vowels such as /i/ (as in *beat*) and /ɛ/ (as in *bet*) because they are both produced with the tongue positioned high and in the front of the mouth. Thus, it would be easier to distinguish between vowels such as /u/ (as in *boot*), produced with the tongue positioned high and in the back of the mouth, and /æ/ (as in *bat*), produced with the tongue positioned low and in the front of the mouth. In addition, as previously mentioned, perception of a sound may also be affected by factors such as the location of the target sound in the word and the amount of support provided by the context.

USiNG THiS BOOK

Assessing Phonological Awareness

Students' awareness of phonemes in academic and humor items can be informally measured before and after they use the intervention materials in *Sounds Like Fun.* Randomly select three items from each unit's Warm-up Activities before intervention and three different items from these units after intervention. In addition, randomly select three to five items from the Phonological Humor Activities throughout the book. If students respond correctly to most of the items, phonological awareness skills are probably at an acceptable level. Although this is an informal assessment, responses can be compared with those in the answer keys, if desired, to determine their adequacy. In addition, classroom teachers can generally provide information regarding students' understanding and use of the phonological elements of language by examining students' reading and writing assignments.

Phonological awareness also can be assessed by using the following commercially developed tools:

- *Lindamood Auditory Conceptualization Test* by Lindamond and Lindamood (1979). This is an individually administered criterion-referenced test that measures the ability to: 1) discriminate one phoneme from another and 2) segment a spoken word into its constituent phonemic units. It can be used for children, adolescents, or adults.

- *The Phonological Awareness Test 2* by Robertson and Salter (2007). This is an updated version of an individually administered standardized test introduced in 1997. The subtests, generally arranged in a developmental sequence, assess a wide variety of tasks correlated with early reading and spelling achievement. It is appropriate for children ages 5–9 years.

- Test of Phonological Awareness-Second Edition: Plus (TOPA-2+) by Torgesen and Bryant (2004). This revision of the Test of Phonological Awareness is a group-administered, norm-referenced measure of phonological awareness. TOPA-2+ measures young children's ability to isolate individual phonemes in spoken words and to understand the relationships between letters and phonemes in English. There are two versions: Kindergarten and Early Elementary, covering grades 1–3.

- Comprehensive Test of Phonological Processing (CTOPP) by Wagner, Torgesen, and Rashotte (1999). This test uses a variety of tasks to assess a student's ability to perceive and manipulate the sounds that make up words. There are forms for ages 5–6 years and for ages 7–21 years.

Presenting the Intervention Materials

The intervention activities in *Sounds Like Fun* are appropriate for one-to-one or group interactions. The first page of each unit includes facilitator notes, with examples of and suggestions for the activities. The example should be presented orally before students complete the activities. This will give students the opportunity to hear acceptable responses before attempting the activities on their own.

Warm-up Activities precede the following four types of Phonological Humor Activities:

- Take Away a Consonant Sound

- Change a Consonant Sound

- Change a Vowel Sound

- Add a Consonant Sound (Note: Warm-up Activities are divided into single consonants and consonant clusters.)

The Warm-up Activities within a unit are not presented in any developmental hierarchy; thus, these activities may be completed in any order.

Each Warm-up Activity has eight Think It Through tasks, in which students hear or read a clue (depending on the mode of presentation selected) and determine the word being described (e.g., Add a consonant sound to make the word *eel* a word that means "the covering of a banana") and two Write a Riddle tasks, in which students create a riddle for others to solve (e.g., Take away a consonant sound to make the word *wink* a word that means "_____").

The Warm-up Activities are followed by review activities, which provide additional phonological awareness practice. Using the eight boldface Think It Through words from the Warm-up Activity that students have just completed, students find rhyming words; match sounds to words; segment words; and identify, manipulate, and blend sounds. The review activities should be read to the students as an oral exercise.

Once the Warm-up Activities for a unit are completed, students should engage in the Phonological Humor Activities. Each page presents three jokes or riddles, each followed by four questions that probe phonological awareness and understanding. The Phonological Humor Activities within a unit are not presented in any developmental hierarchy; thus, these activities may also be completed in any order.

When presenting the Warm-up Activities, Phonological Humor Activities, or Challenge Activities, use the following guidelines:

1. Duplicate the activity pages and distribute one to each student. As an alternative, make transparencies of the activities and use them on an overhead projector.

2. Read the facilitator notes and work together with students to orally complete the examples. Upon beginning a new unit, facilitate a discussion about the nature of the sound change causing the humor.

3. Decide whether to read and complete the items together or to have students read and complete them alone. This decision should be based on what would be most beneficial for each student. Consider reading skills, visual acuity, and so forth.

4. Decide whether responses to stimulus items will be written or oral. Again, this decision should be based on what is best for each student. The mode of presenting the items (on duplicated student pages or on an overhead projector) also will affect this decision.

5. Introduce the activities by discussing why it is necessary to look at both sound changes in general and sound changes causing humor. Say to students, "We are going to be looking at jokes and riddles to see how they are made funny by adding,

changing, or taking away a sound. Can you think of any reasons why we should learn how sound changes affect the meaning of words in jokes and riddles?" Allow students to generate responses. Suggest or reiterate the following reasons:

- We will be able to laugh at and enjoy the jokes and riddles that have this kind of humor.
- We feel more like a part of the group if we understand the kind of humor others use.
- We may prevent feeling embarrassed or insecure about participating in conversations with friends and family if we don't understand what everyone else seems to understand.

6. Discuss the responses to each item. If desired, compare students' responses with those in the answer key on pages 127–144. Although a prototype of correct responses is provided, students may differ in their determination and explanation of the most salient context clues. A range of acceptable responses may be given for any item. For example, for the question "Who lives in the ocean, has tentacles, and is quick on the draw?" and answer "Billy the Squid," one response to question c, "Which words or phrases give you a clue why the funny word was used?" and question d, "Explain why the funny word was used," is the following: *"lives in the ocean, tentacles and quick on the draw. Kid was changed because a squid live in the ocean and has tentacles, and Billy the Kid, which sounds like Billy the Squid, was a western outlaw."* An alternate but equally correct response is the following: *"tentacles and quick on the draw. Kid was changed because a squid has tentacles, and Billy the Kid, an outlaw of the old west, was known for his ability to draw his gun very quickly."* Judging correctness of students' responses is left to the discretion of the facilitator.

Teaching with This Resource

Before presenting the activities in *Sounds Like Fun*, take a moment to review the following suggestions:

Verbal Mediation
In the early stages of intervention, offer a great deal of ongoing verbal mediation. Use the example items on the facilitator page at the beginning of each unit to discuss possible responses to each question so that a correct pattern of response is set for the intervention items. When discussing an item such as "Who is the most badly behaved superhero?...Bratman," for example, ask students to carefully look at the joke and find the word that has a sound added to it. If the word *Bratman* is not selected, suggest examining the joke closely for clues. If the correct word still is not selected, say *Bratman*, and ask what the real word could be. Remind students that the word *Bratman* has a sound added to it. If *Batman* is not given, steer students to the location of the sound addition (e.g., "Look at the beginning of the word *Bratman*"). If the correct word still is not given, say *Batman*, and ask students to look at the joke and find the words that give them a clue why it was changed in this way. If students do not respond *"badly behaved superhero,"* discuss the fact that a brat is someone who behaves badly, and Batman is a superhero. Point out that the humor in the joke is caused by the use of the word *Bratman* for *Batman* because they sound alike. Continue to offer verbal mediation as long as necessary.

Rhyming

Given that the joke and riddle items are based on sound changes, the word changed for humorous effect and the word it could be often rhyme. For example, in the item "Why did the germ cross the microscope?...To get to the other slide," *slide* and *side* rhyme. Point out the rhyming quality in those items where it occurs.

Vocabulary

Before attempting the humor items in any section, you may want to examine them. If you feel any words may be unfamiliar to students, be prepared to discuss their meaning. It is advisable to have an age-appropriate dictionary and a thesaurus available for students.

World Knowledge

The extent of students' world knowledge affects their ability to understand humor created by one or more phonological changes. For example, in the item "Why do they say George Washington was an orphan?...He was the foundling father of his country," to discern which word has the sound change causing the humor, students would have to know that often Washington is referred to as the founding father of the United States of America. To ensure understanding of humor items, such as in this example, provide information to fill in the gaps in students' world knowledge base.

Context Clues

Remind students that the interpretation of an item often depends on the context in which it is embedded. Always look for any context clues that may be available.

Thinking Aloud

Have students think aloud when attempting to figure out a humor item. In this way, context clues can be identified and discussed. For example, for the item "What do you call a clam that doesn't share?...Shellfish," students should state that the word *clam* and the phrase *doesn't share* give the best clues. If not, point out these context clues and ask students to discuss why the words *shellfish* and *selfish* were used. Provide assistance if students do not think of the following reasons: 1) a clam is a shellfish; 2) when someone doesn't share, he or she is called *selfish*; and 3) *shellfish* sounds like *selfish*. Ukrainetz (2006) highly recommended this think-aloud strategy as a way of showing the child how to analyze the sound structure of language. This kind of modeled analysis and guided practice leads to or triggers the child's critical insights that make possible independent analysis.

A Response-Finding Strategy

For the Warm-up or Additional Activities, if the definition in an item is not a sufficient clue for students to determine the sound change required, ask students to try the following strategy for those items that have a rhyming base: "Go through the alphabet until you find a word that both sounds like the word to be changed and could be a likely response. For example, for the item "Change a consonant sound in the word *lash* to make a word that means 'What you get when you have the measles,'" try *bash, cash, dash, gash, hash, lash, mash,* and so forth, until you find the word *rash*.

Explanation Tasks

To answer question d in the Phonological Humor Activities, students must explain why the sound change was made. It may be easier for students to explain this orally, rather than writing out a full explanation. Decide what is best for each student.

Sound-Symbol Correspondence

Stress the difference between a sound and the letter(s) that symbolize the sound. Discuss how some sounds can be represented by different alphabetic symbols (e.g., /f/ can be represented by *f* (as in *fun*), *ph* (as in *phone*), or *gh* (as in lau*gh*)). Frequently, there is not a one-to-one correspondence between the number of sounds in a word and the number of letters. To illustrate this point, compare words such as *cat* and *caught*. *Cat* (kæt) has three sounds and three letters and *caught* (kɔt) has three sounds and six letters.

Spelling Changes

Some items have a sound change that results in a radical spelling change of the target word. For example, in the item "What disease do racing cars get?...Vroomatism," the joke is formed by changing the word *rheumatism* to *vroomatism*. In those instances when such spelling changes occur, discuss the nature of the change and, if necessary, assist with the spelling.

Effect of the Nature and Position of Sound

Students' understanding of the humor items may be affected by the particular sound in each item and its position within the target word. For example, in the item "What do canaries say on Halloween?...'Trick or tweet,'" the sound substitution of /w/ for /r/ is a fairly common one, often used by young children. In the item "What do you get if you cross a clock and a chicken?...An alarm cluck," the sound change for the word *cluck* is from /ʌ/ to /ɑ/ and therefore may be somewhat more difficult. If the sound change occurs in the medial or final position of a word, rather than the initial position, it may be more difficult to detect (e.g., "Why was the fireplace in the hospital?...Because it had a hearth attack"). In the item "Some folks say that fleas are black, but I know that's not so, 'cause Mary had a little lamb with fleas as white as snow," the difference between the word-final sound in *fleas* and *fleece* is merely one of voicing and may not be easily perceived.

Figurative Language and Other Familiar Expressions

For several of the items, the sound change involves one of the words in an idiomatic expression or a proverb. For example, "Ellen: My husband's name is Ed. If I have a son, should I name him Ed also? SABRINA: Sure. Everyone knows two Eds are better than one." ("Two heads are better than one.") Discuss the meaning of such expressions, or have students use an idiom or proverb dictionary (see the appendix). Other familiar expressions such as "I forgot your name but your face is familiar" are the basis of many target word changes and should be pointed out to students.

Relating Activities to Everyday Life

Point out materials such as T-shirts, billboards, bumper stickers, comic strips, items in books of jokes and riddles, and so forth that have sound changes as their basis for humor. Have students look at these types of materials to find additional items that are based on the addition, substitution, or deletion of a sound in a word to change meaning. Also, students who need to improve their metaphonological skills are more likely to be successful when they recognize the relevance of the intervention activities. Ask students, "Can you think of any ways in which knowing about sounds in words can be helpful?" Allow students to generate responses.

Suggest or reiterate the following ways:

- It can help us read and write (e.g., when we look carefully at the sounds in a word, we are less likely to confuse similar sounding words, such as *stream* and *steam*).
- It can help us determine what someone with a different dialect is saying.
- It can help us make judgment calls about a word distorted by static (e.g., words spoken over radios or intercom systems).
- It can help us spell words correctly during writing tasks.
- It can help us understand and enjoy comments in newspapers, magazines, television programs, and commercials that are based on sound changes (e.g., Scientists working on the spaceship went out to launch).
- It can help us understand and enjoy signs on stores, billboards, bumper stickers, and T-shirts that are based on sound changes (e.g., Name of a flower shop: Petal Pushers).

Activities to Enhance Phoneme Awareness

When assessment shows that a student has difficulty with the basic phonological skills listed, and consequently the activities in *Sounds Like Fun*, consider using the following activities described by Blachman (1991) and Surdak-Upright (1998) to enhance fundamental phonological awareness skills:

Sound Categorization (Bradley & Bryant, 1983, 1985)

Teach the student to categorize or group pictures of objects on the basis of shared sounds. For example, *hen* could be grouped with *men* and *pen* because they rhyme. *Hen* could also be grouped with *hat* and *hill* because they share the initial sound; *hen* could be grouped with *pin* and *sun* because they share the final sound; and *hen* could be grouped with *leg* and *net* because they share the medial sound. Place several picture cards that rhyme or that share a sound in the initial, middle, or final position on a table, along with one picture that does not share this sound. Ask the student to identify the odd one out and to explain his or her choice. Plastic letters that represent each sound can be used, provided the letters in the word have only one option of sound–letter correspondence. Plastic letters allow the student to see, for example, that when *hen* is changed to *pen*, only one letter needs to be changed.

Phoneme Segmentation (Ball & Blachman, 1988, 1991)

Teach the student to represent the sounds in one-, two-, and three-phoneme words by using disks and other manipulatives such as tiles, buttons, or blocks. Each sound is represented with one disk.

Laminate an 8½ by 11-inch piece of paper, if possible, for durability and ease of movement of the disks. Using one finger, move the disk from the top half of the paper to the bottom, having the student say the sound as the disk is moved. Initially, select words that begin with continuous-sound letters, such as *s*, *f*, or *l*, so that they can be held with a minimum of distortion. Pronounce the words slowly (e.g., "sss-uuu-nnn") and have the student move one disk per sound. Stop consonants, such as *b*, *k*, or *t*, can then be segmented. (As an option, have the student practice saying the target word slowly while at the same time holding up one finger to represent each sound in the word.)

Metalinguistic Games (Lundberg et al., 1988; Surdak-Upright, 1998)   Start with rhyming activities. (Dr. Seuss books are an excellent source of rhyming materials.) Engage the student in activities such as the following: "Say a word that rhymes with *top"* (e.g., *pop, hop,* and *mop*); Which of these words sound alike?" (e.g., *wet, mat, hit,* or *pet*); or "Which of these words does not sound like the others?" (e.g., *rock, lock, sock,* or *bat*)." Model each task before asking the student to respond.

Progress to segmentation of sentences into word units. For example, after modeling the task, ask the student to use one block per word to show how many words are in a spoken sentence (e.g., *"Mary had a little lamb"* = 5 blocks).

Next, segment multisyllabic words into syllables. For example, after modeling the task, ask the student to use one block per syllable to show how many syllables are in a multisyllabic word (*lollipop* = 3 blocks).

Help the student identify the initial phonemes in words, starting with spoken words that begin with continuous sounds (e.g., *sap* = /s/, *fit* = /f/, *lip* = /l/). Progress to spoken words that begin with stop sounds (e.g., *top* = /t/, *cat* = /k/, *dog* = /d/).

Then, help the student segment the phonemes in a spoken word. For example, ask the student to say quickly a word that is spoken slowly (e.g., *b-a-t* would become *bat*). Then, ask the student to say slowly a word that is spoken quickly (e.g., *fat* would become *f-a-t*).

Finally, help the student progress to segmenting phonemes in items that contain two- and then three-phoneme blends (e.g., *glass, street*).

As you implement the ideas in *Sounds Like Fun* with your students, watch for those who need practice with more basic skills, as well as those who may be able to progress more rapidly to increasingly challenging items. Point out how phonological awareness has an impact on students' lives whenever opportunities arise. Finally, keep the fun alive using the jokes and riddles in *Sounds Like Fun*. After all, humor involves playing with words, not working with them.

A WORD ABOUT THE BiRD

The puffin, which inhabits several pages of this book, is considered by many bird lovers to be very cute and humorous looking. I wholeheartedly agree and hope P.J. Puffin tickles your fancy as well as that of your students.

To my children, Lauren, Jeff, and Suzanne,
and in memory of my sister, Glady

TAKE AWAY A CONSONANT SOUND

WARM-UP ACTIVITIES

FACILITATOR NOTES

Using the *Warm-up Activities* in this unit, students practice deleting a consonant sound from a word to make a new word that fits a given definition. These activities are provided to prepare students for the *Phonological Humor Activities* on pages 13–26.

Using the *Think It Through* activities, students solve a puzzle. They use their world knowledge to determine the word that is appropriate for a given definition. Because more than one letter can represent a single sound (e.g., /n/ in *kneel*), students should focus on how words are pronounced rather than spelled. If desired, compare students' responses with those in the answer key (see page 129).

The *Write a Riddle* activities give students a chance to create some riddles of their own. Students think of a consonant sound to delete from the boldface word to make it into a different word. Then they write their own clue so that someone else can solve the riddle. Encourage students to swap their Write a Riddle activities to solve each others' riddles.

A review page follows each warm-up page. The purpose of the review activities is to provide additional phonological awareness practice. Using the boldface words from the preceding Warm-Up Activity, students find rhyming words; match sounds to words; segment words; and identify, manipulate, and blend sounds. The review activities should be conducted orally.

Complete the following examples conducted orally with the students. This will give them the opportunity to practice the two types of Warm-up Activities before trying some activities on their own. Provide as much or as little support as necessary for the activities.

THINK IT THROUGH

Directions: Take away a consonant sound to make the word:

1. *ties,* a word that means "the parts of your body used to see" (*eyes*)
2. *glove,* a word that means "to have strong affection for another person" (*love*)

WRITE A RIDDLE

Directions: Take away a consonant sound to make the word:

1. *peak,* a word that means "_____"
   Example answer: "a small, round, green vegetable" (*pea*)
2. *gray,* a word that means "_____"
   Example answer: "a beam of sunlight" (*ray*)

TAKE AWAY A CONSONANT SOUND

WARM-UP ACTIVITY 1

THINK IT THROUGH

Directions: Take away a consonant sound to make the word:

1. *mice,* a word that means "frozen water" _____

2. *boil,* a word that means "something used to fry food" _____

3. *tend,* a word that means "another word for *finish*" _____

4. *peel,* a word that means "a type of sea creature" _____

5. *mold,* a word that means "the opposite of young" _____

6. *near,* a word that means "a part of your head used to hear" _____

7. *pill,* a word that means "another word for *sick*" _____

8. *moat,* a word that means "a type of grain" _____

WRITE A RIDDLE

Directions: Write your own riddle on the long line. Then, exchange riddles with a friend and have him or her write the answers on the short line below each clue. Take away a consonant sound to make the word:

1. *wink,* a word that means "_____"

   _____

2. *howl,* a word that means "_____"

   _____

UNIT 1

TAKE AWAY A CONSONANT SOUND

WARM-UP ACTIVITY 1 REVIEW

Directions to Facilitator

Read the following items to students. Have them respond orally. When appropriate, pause to wait for students to respond.

1. Look at the eight boldface Think It Through words in Warm-up Activity 1. Which word rhymes with *feel*?

2. Say /m/ /oo/ /t/. Blend those sounds together. Which word do they make?

3. Say *boil.* What is the last sound in that word?

4. Say *near.* What is the first sound in that word?

5. Look at the eight boldface Think It Through words in Warm-up Activity 1. Which word rhymes with *hill*?

6. Say *tend.* Now say the four sounds in *tend.*

7. Say /m/ /oo/ /l/ /d/. Blend those sounds together. Which word do they make?

8. Say *mice.* Now say *ice.* What sound was not included in the second word?

5

WARM-UP ACTIVITY 2

THINK IT THROUGH

Directions: Take away a consonant sound to make the word:

1. *fleet,* a word that means "to run away from danger" _____

2. *line,* a word that means "to say something that is not true" _____

3. *bake,* a word that means "a small body of water" _____

4. *baste,* a word that means "a deep, low-pitched voice" _____

5. *type,* a word that means "an article of clothing worn around the neck"
   _____

6. *feet,* a word that means "a charge for a service" _____

7. *float,* a word that means "to move smoothly and continuously" _____

8. *goat,* a word that means "to proceed, to move along" _____

WRITE A RIDDLE

Directions: Write your own riddle on the long line. Then, exchange riddles with a friend and have him or her write the answers on the short line below each clue. Take away a consonant sound to make the word:

1. *spine,* a word that means "_____"
   _____

2. *cart,* a word that means "_____"
   _____

UNIT 1

TAKE AWAY A CONSONANT SOUND

WARM-UP ACTIVITY 2 REVIEW

Directions to Facilitator

Read the following items to students. Have them respond orally. When appropriate, pause to wait for students to respond.

1. Say *baste.* Now say the four sounds in *baste.*

2. Say *line.* Now say *lie.* What sound was not included in the second word?

3. Say *type.* Now say *tie.* What sound was not included in the second word?

4. Say /f/ /l/ /o͞o/ /t/. Blend those sounds together. Which word do they make?

5. Say *fleet.* What is the last sound in that word?

6. Say *goat.* Now say the three sounds in *goat.*

7. Look at the eight boldface Think It Through words in Warm-up Activity 2. Which word rhymes with *take*?

8. Say *feet.* What is the first sound in that word?

UNIT 1

TAKE AWAY A CONSONANT SOUND

WARM-UP ACTIVITY 3

THINK IT THROUGH

Directions: Take away a consonant sound to make the word:

1. *flap,* a word that means "something you have when you sit down" _____

2. *strip,* a word that means "a journey" _____

3. *twine,* a word that means "a beverage made from grapes" _____

4. *flake,* a word that means "a body of water" _____

5. *praise,* a word that means "to lift up or elevate" _____

6. *slate,* a word that means "the opposite of early" _____

7. *scold,* a word that means "the way you feel when the temperature is below freezing"

   _____

8. *spoke,* a word that means "to jab at someone" _____

WRITE A RIDDLE

Directions: Write your own riddle on the long line. Then, exchange riddles with a friend and have him or her write the answers on the short line below each clue. Take away a consonant sound to make the word:

1. *strain,* a word that means "_____"

   _____

2. *blocks,* a word that means "_____"

   _____

UNIT 1 — TAKE AWAY A CONSONANT SOUND

WARM-UP ACTIVITY 3 REVIEW

Directions to Facilitator

Read the following items to students. Have them respond orally. When appropriate, pause to wait for students to respond.

1. Look at the eight boldface Think It Through words in Warm-up Activity 3. Which word rhymes with *maze*?

2. Say *spoke.* What is the last sound in that word?

3. Say *flake.* Now say the four sounds in *flake.*

4. Say *flap.* Now say *lap.* What sound was not included in the second word?

5. Say /s/ /k/ /oʊ/ /l/ /d/. Blend those sounds together. Which word do they make?

6. Say *slate.* What is the first sound in that word?

7. Look at the eight boldface Think It Through words in Warm-up Activity 3. Which word rhymes with *mine*?

8. Say *strip.* Now say the five sounds in *strip.*

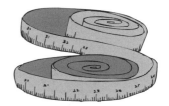

TAKE AWAY A CONSONANT SOUND

WARM-UP ACTIVITY 4

THINK IT THROUGH

Directions: Take away a consonant sound to make the word:

1. *mall,* a word that means "the opposite of none" _____

2. *feet,* a word that means "to consume food" _____

3. *rail,* a word that means "to feel poorly" _____

4. *click,* a word that means "what you do when you eat an ice-cream cone"

    _____

5. *folk,* a word that means "a kind of tree" _____

6. *cinch,* a word that means "a unit of measurement" _____

7. *bring,* a word that means "a band worn around a finger" _____

8. *train,* a word that means "the water that falls from clouds" _____

WRITE A RIDDLE

Directions: Write your own riddle on the long line. Then, exchange riddles with a friend and have him or her write the answers on the short line below each clue. Take away a consonant sound to make the word:

1. *place,* a word that means "_____"

    _____

2. *bout,* a word that means "_____"

    _____

TAKE AWAY A CONSONANT SOUND

WARM-UP ACTIVITY 4 REVIEW

Directions to Facilitator

Read the following items to students. Have them respond orally. When appropriate, pause to wait for students to respond.

1. Say /k/ /l/ /ɪ/ /k/. blend those sounds together. Which word do they make?

2. Look at the eight boldface Think It Through words in Warm-Up Activity 4. Which word rhymes with *sing*?

3. Say *mall.* What is the last sound in that word?

4. Say *rail.* Now say *ail.* What sound was not included in the second word?

5. Say *feet.* What is the first sound in that word?

6. Say *cinch.* Now say the four sounds in *cinch.*

7. Say *train.* Now say *rain.* What sound was not included in the second word?

8. Say /f/ /ʊ/ /k/. Blend those sounds together. Which word do they make?

PHONOLOGICAL HUMOR ACTIVITIES

FACILITATOR NOTES

The *Phonological Humor Activities* in this unit contain words with a consonant sound added to another consonant sound to make the item into a joke. Students must take away a consonant sound from the funny word to determine what the real word is. Because more than one letter can represent a single sound, students should focus on how words are pronounced rather than spelled.

Complete the following examples orally with the students. This will give them the opportunity to hear acceptable responses to the questions. Because the word with a consonant sound added and the funny word always sound similar, this fact alone will not be a complete answer to question d. Students should rely on their own world knowledge of the subject to explain the relationship between the words.

An answer key is provided for the activities (see pages 129–132). The answers are only suggestions. The correctness of students' responses is left to the discretion of the facilitator.

EXAMPLE 1

Q: How do fireflies start a race?

A: "Ready, set, glow!"

a. Which word in the answer makes the joke funny? (*glow*)

b. What do you think the real word is? (*go*)

c. Which words or phrases give you a clue why the funny word was used? (*fireflies* and *race*)

d. Explain why the funny word was used. (Fireflies glow, which sounds like *go,* and a race is started by saying "Ready, set, go!")

EXAMPLE 2

Q: Who is the most badly behaved superhero?

A: Bratman.

a. Which word makes the joke funny? (*Bratman*)

b. What do you think the real word is? (*Batman*)

c. Which words or phrases give you a clue why the funny word was used? (*badly behaved superhero*)

d. Explain why the funny word was used. (A *brat* is someone who behaves badly, and *Batman* is a superhero.)

UNIT 1	TAKE AWAY A CONSONANT SOUND

PHONOLOGICAL HUMOR ACTIVITY 1

Directions: Answer the questions below each item.

1. **Q: What is the first thing a little gorilla learns in school?**

    A: The Ape B Cs.

    a.   Which word in the answer makes the joke funny? _____

    b.   What do you think the real word is? _____

    c.   Which words or phrases give you a clue why the funny word was used? _____

    d.   Explain why the funny word was used. _____

    _____

2. **Q: What did the rabbit want to do when he grew up?**

    A: He wanted to join the Hare Force.

    a.   Which word in the answer makes the joke funny? _____

    b.   What do you think the real word is? _____

    c.   Which words or phrases give you a clue why the funny word was used? _____

    d.   Explain why the funny word was used. _____

    _____

3. **Q: What western hero made the most noise at dinner?**

    A: Wyatt Burp.

    a.   Which word in the answer makes the joke funny? _____

    b.   What do you think the real word is? _____

    c.   Which words or phrases give you a clue why the funny word was used? _____

    d.   Explain why the funny word was used. _____

    _____

Sounds Like Fun: Activities for Developing Phonological Awareness, Revised Edition

TAKE AWAY A CONSONANT SOUND

PHONOLOGICAL HUMOR ACTIVITY 2

Directions: Answer the questions below each item.

1. **Q: In what sport do mice athletes excel?**
   A: Mice hockey.

   a. Which word in the answer makes the joke funny? _____

   b. What do you think the real word is? _____

   c. Which words or phrases give you a clue why the funny word was used? _____

   d. Explain why the funny word was used. _____

   _____

2. **Q: How do the newest wigs from Asia arrive?**
   A: By hair mail.

   a. Which word in the answer makes the joke funny? _____

   b. What do you think the real word is? _____

   c. Which words or phrases give you a clue why the funny word was used? _____

   d. Explain why the funny word was used. _____

   _____

3. **Q: When does a tadpole wear little, pink satin slippers?**
   A: During her toad-dancing lessons.

   a. Which word in the answer makes the joke funny? _____

   b. What do you think the real word is? _____

   c. Which words or phrases give you a clue why the funny word was used? _____

   d. Explain why the funny word was used. _____

   _____

UNIT 1

TAKE AWAY A CONSONANT SOUND

PHONOLOGICAL HUMOR ACTIVITY 3

Directions: Answer the questions below each item.

1. **Q: Where do you send a frog to get glasses?**
   A: To a hoptometrist.

   a.   Which word in the answer makes the joke funny? _____

   b.   What do you think the real word is? _____

   c.   Which words or phrases give you a clue why the funny word was used? _____

   d.   Explain why the funny word was used. _____

   _____

2. **Q: What book tells you all about chickens?**
   A: A hencyclopedia.

   a.   Which word makes the joke funny? _____

   b.   What do you think the real word is? _____

   c.   Which words or phrases give you a clue why the funny word was used? _____

   d.   Explain why the funny word was used. _____

   _____

3. **Q: Whose name is mentioned in "The Star-Spangled Banner"?**
   A: José Canusi.

   a.   Which words make the joke funny? _____

   b.   What do you think the real words are? _____

   c.   Which words or phrases give you a clue why the funny words were used? _____

   d.   Explain why the funny words were used. _____

   _____

TAKE AWAY A CONSONANT SOUND

PHONOLOGICAL HUMOR ACTIVITY 4

Directions: Answer the questions below each item.

1. **Q: How does a pig go to the hospital?**

   A: In a hambulance.

   a. Which word makes the joke funny? _____

   b. What do you think the real word is? _____

   c. Which words or phrases give you a clue why the funny word was used? _____

   d. Explain why the funny word was used. _____

   _____

2. **Q: What would you see at a chicken show?**

   A: Hentertainment.

   a. Which word makes the joke funny? _____

   b. What do you think the real word is? _____

   c. Which words or phrases give you a clue why the funny word was used? _____

   d. Explain why the funny word was used. _____

   _____

3. **Q: What is sweet and sour and kicks?**

   A: Kung food.

   a. Which word in the answer makes the joke funny? _____

   b. What do you think the real word is? _____

   c. Which words or phrases give you a clue why the funny word was used? _____

   d. Explain why the funny word was used. _____

   _____

TAKE AWAY A CONSONANT SOUND

PHONOLOGICAL HUMOR ACTIVITY 5

Directions: Answer the questions below each item.

1. **Q: What do you call witches who live together?**

   A: Broommates.

   a. Which word makes the joke funny? _____

   b. What do you think the real word is? _____

   c. Which words or phrases give you a clue why the funny word was used? _____

   d. Explain why the funny word was used. _____

   _____

2. **Q: Which fairy smelled bad?**

   A: Stinkerbell.

   a. Which word makes the joke funny? _____

   b. What do you think the real word is? _____

   c. Which words or phrases give you a clue why the funny word was used? _____

   d. Explain why the funny word was used. _____

   _____

3. **A shoplifter is a person who has the gift of grab.**

   a. Which word in the sentence makes the joke funny? _____

   b. What do you think the real word is? _____

   c. Which words or phrases give you a clue why the funny word was used? _____

   d. Explain why the funny word was used. _____

   _____

PHONOLOGICAL HUMOR ACTIVITY 6

Directions: Answer the questions below each item.

1. **Q: Why do they say George Washington was an orphan?**
    A: He was the foundling father of his country.

    a. Which word in the answer makes the joke funny? _____

    b. What do you think the real word is? _____

    c. Which words or phrases give you a clue why the funny word was used? _____

    d. Explain why the funny word was used. _____

    _____

2. **When signing a contract, always read the fine print carefully; there may be a clause for suspicion.**

    a. Which word in the sentence makes the joke funny? _____

    b. What do you think the real word is? _____

    c. Which words or phrases give you a clue why the funny word was used? _____

    d. Explain why the funny word was used. _____

    _____

3. **Q: What do ghouls have for breakfast?**
    A: Scream of Wheat.

    a. Which word in the answer makes the joke funny? _____

    b. What do you think the real word is? _____

    c. Which words or phrases give you a clue why the funny word was used? _____

    d. Explain why the funny word was used. _____

    _____

TAKE AWAY A CONSONANT SOUND

PHONOLOGICAL HUMOR ACTIVITY 7

Directions: Answer the questions below each item.

1. **Q: Who performs the operations in a fish hospital?**

   A: The head sturgeon.

   a.   Which word in the answer makes the joke funny? _____

   b.   What do you think the real word is? _____

   c.   Which words or phrases give you a clue why the funny word was used? _____

   d.   Explain why the funny word was used. _____

   _____

2. **After reading a book she didn't like, the critic said, "This book should be on the bestsmeller list."**

   a.   Which word in the sentence makes the joke funny? _____

   b.   What do you think the real word is? _____

   c.   Which words or phrases give you a clue why the funny word was used? _____

   d.   Explain why the funny word was used. _____

   _____

3. **Q: Do zombies like being dead?**

   A: Of corpse.

   a.   Which word makes the joke funny? _____

   b.   What do you think the real word is? _____

   c.   Which words or phrases give you a clue why the funny word was used? _____

   d.   Explain why the funny word was used. _____

   _____

TAKE AWAY A CONSONANT SOUND

PHONOLOGICAL HUMOR ACTIVITY 8

Directions: Answer the questions below each item.

1. **Q: What does a baseball catcher sing when wearing a mitt?**
   A: Glove songs.

   a. Which word in the answer makes the joke funny? _____

   b. What do you think the real word is? _____

   c. Which words or phrases give you a clue why the funny word was used? _____

   d. Explain why the funny word was used. _____

   _____

2. **Q: What is another title for an editor?**
   A: Fiddler on the Proof.

   a. Which word in the answer makes the joke funny? _____

   b. What do you think the real word is? _____

   c. Which words or phrases give you a clue why the funny word was used? _____

   d. Explain why the funny word was used. _____

   _____

3. **Q: What did one skunk say to the other skunk when they were cornered?**
   A: "Let us spray."

   a. Which word in the answer makes the joke funny? _____

   b. What do you think the real word is? _____

   c. Which words or phrases give you a clue why the funny word was used? _____

   d. Explain why the funny word was used. _____

   _____

TAKE AWAY A CONSONANT SOUND

PHONOLOGICAL HUMOR ACTIVITY 13

Directions: Answer the questions below each item.

1. **Q: What kind of thief steals meat?**

   A: A hamburglar.

   a. Which word makes the joke funny? _____

   b. What do you think the real word is? _____

   c. Which words or phrases give you a clue why the funny word was used? _____

   d. Explain why the funny word was used. _____

   _____

2. **Q: Why did the germ cross the microscope?**

   A: To get to the other slide.

   a. Which word in the answer makes the joke funny? _____

   b. What do you think the real word is? _____

   c. Which words or phrases give you a clue why the funny word was used? _____

   d. Explain why the funny word was used. _____

   _____

3. **Q: What did the referee say before the ghost boxing match?**

   A: "May the best frighter win."

   a. Which word in the answer makes the joke funny? _____

   b. What do you think the real word is? _____

   c. Which words or phrases give you a clue why the funny word was used? _____

   d. Explain why the funny word was used. _____

   _____

PHONOLOGICAL HUMOR ACTIVITIES

REVIEW AND REFLECTION

1. a. Look through the Phonological Humor Activities you have just finished. Which joke was the easiest for you to understand?

    _____

    b. Why do you think it was the easiest?

    _____

    _____

2. a. Which joke was the hardest for you to understand?

    _____

    b. Why do you think it was the hardest?

    _____

    _____

3. a. Which joke did you think was the funniest?

    _____

    b. Why do you think it was the funniest?

    _____

    _____

4. The activities in this unit are based on taking away a consonant sound. When else have you seen a consonant sound taken away from a word to create humor? (Hint: Think of some T-shirts or signs you have seen.)

    _____

    _____

5. How does knowing about sounds in words help you when you are in school or doing your homework?

    _____

    _____

    _____

UNIT 2

CHANGE A CONSONANT SOUND

WARM-UP ACTIVITIES

FACILITATOR NOTES

Using the *Warm-up Activities* in this unit, students practice substituting a consonant sound in a word to make a new word that fits a given definition. These activities are provided to prepare students for the *Phonological Humor Activities* on pages 39–49.

Using the *Think It Through* activities, students solve a puzzle. They use their world knowledge to determine the word that is appropriate for a given definition. Because more than one letter can represent a single sound (e.g., /n/ in *kneel*), students should focus on how words are pronounced rather than spelled. If desired, compare students' responses with those in the answer key (see page 133).

The *Write a Riddle* activities give students a chance to create some riddles of their own. Students think of a consonant sound to substitute in the boldface word to make it into a different word. Then they write their own clue so that someone else can solve the riddle. Encourage students to swap their Write a Riddle activities to solve each others' riddles.

A review page follows each warm-up page. The purpose of the review activities is to provide additional phonological awareness practice. Using the boldface words from the preceding Warm-Up Activity, students find rhyming words; match sounds to words; segment words; and identify, manipulate, and blend sounds. The review activities should be conducted orally.

Complete the following examples orally with the students. This will give them the opportunity to practice the two types of Warm-up Activities before trying some activities on their own. Provide as much or as little support as necessary for the activities.

THINK IT THROUGH

Directions: Change a consonant sound to make the word:

1. **slot,** a word that means "a stain on clothing" (*spot*)
2. **game,** a word that means "to stare at in astonishment" (*gape*)

WRITE A RIDDLE

Directions: Change a consonant sound to make the word:

1. **pleat,** a word that means "_____"
    Example answer: "icy rain" (*sleet*)
2. **mood,** a word that means "_____"
    Example answer: "an object seen in the sky at night" (*moon*)

THiNK iT THROUGH

Directions: Change a consonant sound to make the word:

1. *tick,* a word that means "ill" _____

2. *night,* a word that means "not heavy" _____

3. *money,* a word that means "a substance made by bees" _____

4. *let,* a word that means "a very fast plane" _____

5. *pound,* a word that means "circular" _____

6. *think,* a word that means "a place to wash your hands." _____

7. *house,* a word that means "a small rodent" _____

8. *pad,* a word that means "unhappy" _____

WRiTE A RiDDLE

Directions: Write your own riddle on the long line. Then, exchange riddles with a friend and have him or her write the answers on the short line below each clue. Change a consonant sound to make the word:

1. *best,* a word that means "_____"
    _____

2. *boat,* a word that means "_____"
    _____

CHANGE A CONSONANT SOUND

WARM-UP ACTIVITY 1 REVIEW

Directions to Facilitator

Read the following items to students. Have them respond orally. When appropriate, pause to wait for students to respond.

1. Say /n/ /ɑɪ/ /t/. Blend those sounds together. Which word do they make?

2. Say *let.* Now say the three sounds in *let.*

3. Say *house.* Now say *mouse.* What sound was different in the second word?

4. Listen to this word: *pound.* Does *pound* end with a /d/ sound?

5. Say *tick.* Now say *sick.* What sound was different in the second word?

6. Say *think.* What is the first sound in that word?

7. Say *pad.* Now say the three sounds in *pad.*

8. Look at the eight boldface Think It Through words in Warm-up Activity 1. Which word rhymes with *sunny*?

UNIT 2

CHANGE A CONSONANT SOUND

WARM-UP ACTIVITY 2

THINK IT THROUGH

Directions: Change a consonant sound to make the word:

1. **trip,** a word that means "something that a magician does" _____

2. **grim,** a word that means "a happy expression" _____

3. **drone,** a word that mean "went somewhere in a car" _____

4. **skid,** a word that means "the outer layer that covers a person's body"
   _____

5. **paid,** a word that means "a leaf in a book" _____

6. **clot,** a word that means "an instrument for telling time" _____

7. **creek,** a word that means "to crawl slowly on all fours" _____

8. **June,** a word that means "the liquid you get from an orange when it is squeezed"
   _____

WRITE A RIDDLE

Directions: Write your own riddle on the long line. Then, exchange riddles with a friend and have him or her write the answers on the short line below each clue. Change a consonant sound to make the word:

1. **gate,** a word that means "_____"
   _____

2. **plop,** a word that means "_____"
   _____

CHANGE A CONSONANT SOUND

WARM-UP ACTIVITY 2 REVIEW

Directions to Facilitator
Read the following items to students. Have them respond orally. When appropriate, pause to wait for students to respond.

1. Listen to this word: *creek.* Does *creek* end with a /g/ sound?

2. Say *drone.* Now say the four sounds in *drone.*

3. Say *trip.* What is the first sound in that word?

4. Look at the eight boldface Think It Through words in Warm-up Activity 2. Which word rhymes with *maid*?

5. Say *grim.* Now say *grin.* What sound was different in the second word?

6. Say /k/ /l/ /ɑ/ /t/. Blend those sounds together. Which word do they make?

7. Say *June.* Now say *juice.* What sound was different in the second word?

8. Say *skid.* What is the last sound in that word?

UNIT 2

CHANGE A CONSONANT SOUND

WARM-UP ACTIVITY 3

THINK IT THROUGH

Directions: Change a consonant sound to make the word:

1.   *stake,* a word that means "a long, slithering creature" _____

2.   *scale,* a word that means "the way bread tastes when it has been around too long"
     _____

3.   *stoke,* a word that means "the vapor that comes out of a chimney" _____

4.   *brush,* a word that means "to become red in the face when embarrassed"
     _____

5.   *stunk,* a word that means "animal that can spray a horrible odor" _____

6.   *smack,* a word that means "a light bite eaten between meals" _____

7.   *crone,* a word that means "an identical copy of something or someone"
     _____

8.   *stout,* a word that means "the place where water comes out of a teapot"
     _____

WRITE A RIDDLE

Directions: Write your own riddle on the long line. Then, exchange riddles with a friend and have him or her write the answers on the short line below each clue. Change a consonant sound to make the word:

1.   *slip,* a word that means "_____"
     _____

2.   *glow,* a word that means "_____"
     _____

Sounds Like Fun: Activities for Developing Phonological Awareness, Revised Edition

UNIT 2 · CHANGE A CONSONANT SOUND

WARM-UP ACTIVITY 3 REVIEW

Directions to Facilitator

Read the following items to students. Have them respond orally. When appropriate, pause to wait for students to respond.

1. Say /s/ /m/ /æ/ /k/. Blend those sounds together. Which word do they make?

2. Look at the eight boldface Think It Through words in Warm-up Activity 3. Which word rhymes with *groan*?

3. Say *brush*. Now say the four sounds in *brush*.

4. Say *stoke*. What is the last sound in *stoke?*

5. Say *stout*. Now say *spout*. What sound was different in the second word?

6. Listen to this word: *stake*. Does stake end with a /k/ sound?

7. Say *stunk*. Now say the five sounds in *stunk*.

8. Look at the eight boldface Think It Through words in Warm-up Activity 3. Which word rhymes with *pale*?

UNIT 2 CHANGE A CONSONANT SOUND

WARM-UP ACTIVITY 4

THINK IT THROUGH

Directions: Change a consonant sound to make the word:

1. **bleed,** a word that means "to produce offspring"_____

2. **mast,** a word that means "a covering used to disguise your face"
   _____

3. **glass,** a word that means "something that has to be mowed"_____

4. **home,** a word that means "a toothed object used to smooth and style hair"
   _____

5. **mix,** a word that means "to repair"_____

6. **dust,** a word that means "the brittle, reddish coating that forms on iron"
   _____

7. **slain,** a word that means "a soiled or discolored spot"_____

8. **tape,** a word that means "the back of the neck"_____

WRITE A RIDDLE

Directions: Write your own riddle on the long line. Then, exchange riddles with a friend and have him or her write the answers on the short line below each clue. Change a consonant sound to make the word:

1. **lash,** a word that means "_____"
   _____

2. **horse,** a word that means "_____"
   _____

CHANGE A CONSONANT SOUND

WARM-UP ACTIVITY 4 REVIEW

Directions to Facilitator

Read the following items to students. Have them respond orally. When appropriate, pause to wait for students to respond.

1. Say *dust.* Now say *rust.* What sound was different in the second word?

2. Say *slain.* What is the last sound in *slain*?

3. Say *glass.* Now say the four sounds in *glass.*

4. Say /m/ /ɪ/ /k/ /s/. Blend those sounds together. Which word do they make?

5. Say *bleed.* Now say *breed.* What sound was different in the second word?

6. Say *home.* What is the first sound in that word?

7. Look at the eight boldface Think It Through words in Warm-up Activity 4. Which word rhymes with *cape*?

8. Listen to this word: *mast.* Does *mast* end with a /d/ sound?

PHONOLOGICAL HUMOR ACTIVITIES

FACILITATOR NOTES

The *Phonological Humor Activities* in this unit contain words with a consonant sound substituted to make the item into a joke. Students must change a consonant sound in the funny word to determine what the real word is. Because more than one letter can represent a single sound, students should focus on how words are pronounced rather than spelled.

Complete the examples below orally with the students. This will give them the opportunity to hear acceptable responses to the questions. Because the word with a consonant sound changed and the funny word always sound similar, this fact alone will not be a complete answer to question d. Students should rely on their own world knowledge of the subject to explain the relationship between the words.

An answer key is provided for the activities (see pages 133–135). The answers are only suggestions. The correctness of students' responses is left to the discretion of the facilitator.

EXAMPLE 1

Q: What is the first thing ghosts do when they get into a car?

A: They fasten their sheet belts.

a.   Which word in the answer makes the riddle funny? (*sheet*)

b.   What do you think the real word is? (*seat*)

c.   Which words or phrases give you a clue why the funny word was used? (*ghosts* and *car*)

d.   Explain why the funny word was used. (Ghosts are often portrayed wearing sheets; when you are in a car, you wear a seat belt; and *sheet* and *seat* sound alike.)

EXAMPLE 2

Q: What do canaries say on Halloween?

A: "Trick or tweet."

a.   Which word in the answer makes the joke funny? (*tweet*)

b.   What do you think the real word is? (*treat*)

c.   Which words or phrases give you a clue why the funny word was used? (*canaries* and *Halloween*)

d.   Explain why the funny word was used. (Canaries say "tweet," which rhymes with *treat;* and on Halloween, children say "*Trick or treat.*")

PHONOLOGICAL HUMOR ACTIVITY 1

Directions: Answer the questions below each item.

1. **Q: What newspaper do cows read?**

   A: *The Daily Moos.*

   a. Which word in the answer makes the joke funny? _____

   b. What do you think the real word is? _____

   c. Which words or phrases give you a clue why the funny word was used? _____

   d. Explain why the funny word was used. _____

   _____

2. **Q: If called by a panther, what should you do?**

   A: Don't anther.

   a. Which word in the answer makes the joke funny? _____

   b. What do you think the real word is? _____

   c. Which words or phrases give you a clue why the funny word was used? _____

   d. Explain why the funny word was used. _____

   _____

3. **Q: What do you call a frozen police officer?**

   A: A copsicle.

   a. Which word makes the joke funny? _____

   b. What do you think the real word is? _____

   c. Which words or phrases give you a clue why the funny word was used? _____

   d. Explain why the funny word was used. _____

   _____

UNIT 2

CHANGE A CONSONANT SOUND

PHONOLOGICAL HUMOR ACTIVITY 2

Directions: Answer the questions below each item.

1. **Q: What did the farmer use to cure his sick hog?**
    A: Oinkment.

    a.   Which word makes the joke funny? _____

    b.   What do you think the real word is? _____

    c.   Which words or phrases give you a clue why the funny word was used? _____

    d.   Explain why the funny word was used. _____

    _____

2. **Said the newborn infant to his mother, "The quarters were a bit cramped, but the womb service was great!"**

    a.   Which word in the sentence makes the joke funny? _____

    b.   What do you think the real word is? _____

    c.   Which words or phrases give you a clue why the funny word was used? _____

    d.   Explain why the funny word was used. _____

    _____

3. **Q: What do you call a clam that doesn't share?**
    A: Shellfish.

    a.   Which word makes the joke funny? _____

    b.   What do you think the real word is? _____

    c.   Which words or phrases give you a clue why the funny word was used? _____

    d.   Explain why the funny word was used. _____

    _____

UNIT 2

CHANGE A CONSONANT SOUND

PHONOLOGICAL HUMOR ACTIVITY 3

Directions: Answer the questions below each item.

1. **Q: What do you do with dogs when you go shopping?**
    A: Leave them in the barking lot.

    a. Which word in the answer makes the joke funny? _____

    b. What do you think the real word is? _____

    c. Which words or phrases give you a clue why the funny word was used? _____

    d. Explain why the funny word was used. _____

    _____

2. **Q: What did the ghost want to do when he grew up?**
    A: He wanted to join the Ghost Guard.

    a. Which word in the answer makes the joke funny? _____

    b. What do you think the real word is? _____

    c. Which words or phrases give you a clue why the funny word was used? _____

    d. Explain why the funny word was used. _____

    _____

3. **Q: Why did the old angel feel very ill?**
    A: He had a harp attack.

    a. Which word in the answer makes the joke funny? _____

    b. What do you think the real word is? _____

    c. Which words or phrases give you a clue why the funny word was used? _____

    d. Explain why the funny word was used. _____

    _____

UNIT 2

CHANGE A CONSONANT SOUND

PHONOLOGICAL HUMOR ACTIVITY 4

Directions: Answer the questions below each item.

1. **Q: What did one racehorse say to the other racehorse?**
    A: "I forget your name, but your pace is familiar."

    a. Which word in the answer makes the joke funny? _____

    b. What do you think the real word is? _____

    c. Which words or phrases give you a clue why the funny word was used? _____

    d. Explain why the funny word was used. _____

    _____

2. **Q: What happened when Count Dracula met a beautiful girl?**
    A: It was love at first bite.

    a. Which word in the answer makes the joke funny? _____

    b. What do you think the real word is? _____

    c. Which words or phrases give you a clue why the funny word was used? _____

    d. Explain why the funny word was used. _____

    _____

3. **Q: What shampoo do mountains use?**
    A: Head and Boulders.

    a. Which word in the answer makes the joke funny? _____

    b. What do you think the real word is? _____

    c. Which words or phrases give you a clue why the funny word was used? _____

    d. Explain why the funny word was used. _____

    _____

UNIT 2

CHANGE A CONSONANT SOUND

PHONOLOGICAL HUMOR ACTIVITY 5

Directions: Answer the questions below each item.

1. **Q: Why does Batman brush his teeth several times a day?**
   A: To prevent bat breath.

   a. Which word in the answer makes the joke funny? _____

   b. What do you think the real word is? _____

   c. Which words or phrases give you a clue why the funny word was used? _____

   d. Explain why the funny word was used. _____

   _____

2. **Some folks say that fleas are black, but I know that's not so,
   'cause Mary had a little lamb with fleas as white as snow.**

   a. Which word in the sentence makes the joke funny? _____

   b. What do you think the real word is? _____

   c. Which words or phrases give you a clue why the funny word was used? _____

   d. Explain why the funny word was used. _____

   _____

3. **Q: What comes in different flavors and colors and makes music?**
   A: Cello pudding.

   a. Which word in the answer makes the joke funny? _____

   b. What do you think the real word is? _____

   c. Which words or phrases give you a clue why the funny word was used? _____

   d. Explain why the funny word was used. _____

   _____

> UNIT 2

CHANGE A CONSONANT SOUND

PHONOLOGICAL HUMOR ACTIVITY 6

Directions: Answer the questions below each item.

1. **Q: What did the boy snake say to the girl snake?**
   A: "Give me a little hiss."

   a. Which word in the answer makes the joke funny? _____

   b. What do you think the real word is? _____

   c. Which words or phrases give you a clue why the funny word was used? _____

   d. Explain why the funny word was used. _____

   _____

2. **Q: What do you give to a sick bird?**
   A: First-aid tweetment.

   a. Which word in the answer makes the joke funny? _____

   b. What do you think the real word is? _____

   c. Which words or phrases give you a clue why the funny word was used? _____

   d. Explain why the funny word was used. _____

   _____

3. **Q: What do you get if you cross cows and ducks?**
   A: Milk and quackers.

   a. Which word in the answer makes the joke funny? _____

   b. What do you think the real word is? _____

   c. Which words or phrases give you a clue why the funny word was used? _____

   d. Explain why the funny word was used. _____

   _____

UNIT 2

CHANGE A CONSONANT SOUND

PHONOLOGICAL HUMOR ACTIVITY 7

Directions: Answer the questions below each item.

1. **Q: What did the mother broom say to her infant broom?**
   A: "Go to sweep, little baby."

   a. Which word in the answer makes the joke funny? _____

   b. What do you think the real word is? _____

   c. Which words or phrases give you a clue why the funny word was used? _____

   d. Explain why the funny word was used. _____

   _____

2. **Q: Why was the fireplace in the hospital?**
   A: Because he had a hearth attack.

   a. Which word in the answer makes the joke funny? _____

   b. What do you think the real word is? _____

   c. Which words or phrases give you a clue why the funny word was used? _____

   d. Explain why the funny word was used. _____

   _____

3. **Q: Why does an exterminator get so much business?**
   A: He makes mouse calls.

   a. Which word in the answer makes the joke funny? _____

   b. What do you think the real word is? _____

   c. Which words or phrases give you a clue why the funny word was used? _____

   d. Explain why the funny word was used. _____

   _____

UNIT 2

CHANGE A CONSONANT SOUND

PHONOLOGICAL HUMOR ACTIVITY 8

Directions: Answer the questions below each item.

1. **Q: What do spiders like with their hamburgers?**
   A: French flies.

   a. Which word in the answer makes the joke funny? _____

   b. What do you think the real word is? _____

   c. Which words or phrases give you a clue why the funny word was used? _____

   d. Explain why the funny word was used. _____

   _____

2. **Q: What do they call someone who sells mobile homes?**
   A: A wheel estate broker.

   a. Which word in the answer makes the joke funny? _____

   b. What do you think the real word is? _____

   c. Which words or phrases give you a clue why the funny word was used? _____

   d. Explain why the funny word was used. _____

   _____

3. **Q: What did one raindrop say to the other raindrop?**
   A: "Two's company, three's a cloud."

   a. Which word in the answer makes the joke funny? _____

   b. What do you think the real word is? _____

   c. Which words or phrases give you a clue why the funny word was used? _____

   d. Explain why the funny word was used. _____

   _____

UNIT 2

CHANGE A CONSONANT SOUND

PHONOLOGICAL HUMOR ACTIVITY 9

Directions: Answer the questions below each item.

1. **Q: What kind of car does an electrician drive?**
   A: A Voltswagon.

   a. Which word makes the joke funny? _____

   b. What do you think the real word is? _____

   c. Which words or phrases give you a clue why the funny word was used? _____

   d. Explain why the funny word was used. _____

   _____

2. **A woman found a rabbit sleeping in her refrigerator. She woke it up and asked, "What are you doing in my refrigerator?" "Isn't this a Westinghouse?" the rabbit asked. "Yes," said the woman. "Well," said the rabbit, "I'm westing."**

   a. Which word in the rabbit's final answer makes the joke funny? _____

   b. What do you think the real word is? _____

   c. Which words or phrases give you a clue why the funny word was used? _____

   d. Explain why the funny word was used. _____

   _____

3. **Q: Why do Eskimos wash their clothes in Tide?**
   A: Because it's too cold to wash out Tide.

   a. Which word in the answer makes the joke funny? _____

   b. What do you think the real word is? _____

   c. Which words or phrases give you a clue why the funny word was used? _____

   d. Explain why the funny word was used. _____

   _____

UNIT 2 CHANGE A CONSONANT SOUND

PHONOLOGICAL HUMOR ACTIVITY 10

Directions: Answer the questions below each item.

1. **Q: Why did the duck win the sharp-shooting contest?**
   A: Because he was a quack shot.

   a. Which word in the answer makes the joke funny? _____

   b. What do you think the real word is? _____

   c. Which words or phrases give you a clue why the funny word was used? _____

   d. Explain why the funny word was used. _____

   _____

2. **Q: What's big, green, and doesn't speak all day?**
   A: The Incredible Sulk.

   a. Which word in the answer makes the joke funny? _____

   b. What do you think the real word is? _____

   c. Which words or phrases give you a clue why the funny word was used? _____

   d. Explain why the funny word was used. _____

   _____

3. **Q: What do you get if you cross a duck and the Fourth of July?**
   A: A firequacker.

   a. Which word makes the joke funny?_____

   b. What do you think the real word is? _____

   c. Which words or phrases give you a clue why the funny word was used? _____

   d. Explain why the funny word was used. _____

   _____

UNIT 2

CHANGE A CONSONANT SOUND

PHONOLOGICAL HUMOR ACTIVITIES

REVIEW AND REFLECTION

1. a. Look through the Phonological Humor Activities you have just finished. Which joke was the easiest for you to understand?

   _____

   b. Why do you think it was the easiest?

   _____

   _____

2. a. Which joke was the hardest for you to understand?

   _____

   b. Why do you think it was the hardest?

   _____

   _____

3. a. Which joke did you think was the funniest?

   _____

   b. Why do you think it was the funniest?

   _____

   _____

4. The activities in this unit are based on changing a consonant sound. When else have you changed a consonant sound to create different words? (Hint: Think of some poetry you have written.)

   _____

   _____

5. How does knowing about sounds in words help you when you are with your friends and family?

   _____

   _____

   _____

UNIT 3

CHANGE A VOWEL SOUND

WARM-UP ACTIVITIES

FACILITATOR NOTES

The *Warm-up Activities* in this unit have students practice substituting a vowel sound in a word to make a new word that fits a given definition. These activities are provided to prepare students for the *Phonological Humor Activities* on pages 63–67.

Using the *Think It Through* activities, students solve a puzzle. They use their world knowledge to determine the word that is appropriate for a given definition. Because more than one letter can represent a single sound (e.g., /n/ in kneel), students should focus on how words are pronounced rather than spelled. If desired, compare students' responses with those in the answer key (see page 136).

The *Write a Riddle* activities give students a chance to create some riddles of their own. Students think of a vowel sound to change in the boldface word to make it into a different word. Then, they write their own clue so that someone else can solve the riddle. Encourage students to swap their Write a Riddle activities to solve each others' riddles.

A review page follows each warm-up page. The purpose of the review activities is to provide additional phonological awareness practice. Using the boldface words from the preceding Warm-Up Activity, students find rhyming words; match sounds to words; segment words; and identify, manipulate, and blend sounds. The review activities should be conducted orally.

Complete the following examples orally with the students. This will give them the opportunity to practice the two types of Warm-up Activities before trying some activities on their own. Provide as much or as little support as necessary for the activities.

THINK IT THROUGH

Directions: Change a vowel sound to make the word:

1. **saint,** a word that means "mailed" (*sent*)
2. **rug,** a word that means "an old, tattered cloth" (*rag*)

WRITE A RIDDLE

Directions: Change a vowel sound to make the word:

1. **bag,** a word that means "_____"
   Example answer: "the opposite of little" (*big*)
2. **load,** a word that means "_____"
   Example answer: "a young boy" (*lad*)

UNIT 3

CHANGE A VOWEL SOUND

WARM-UP ACTIVITY 1

THINK IT THROUGH

Directions: Change a vowel sound to make the word:

1. **ride,** a word that means "something cars drive on" _____

2. **bake,** a word that means "the opposite of front" _____

3. **bought,** a word that means "an object used to hit a baseball" _____

4. **bag,** a word that means "an insect" _____

5. **limp,** a word that means "a device to light a room" _____

6. **trick,** a word that means "a large vehicle" _____

7. **rag,** a word that means "something used to cover a floor" _____

8. **bale,** a word that means "something to put cereal in" _____

WRITE A RIDDLE

Directions: Write your own riddle on the long line. Then, exchange riddles with a friend and have him or her write the answers on the short line below each clue. Change a vowel sound to make the word:

1. **Coke,** a word that means " _____ "

   _____

2. **like,** a word that means " _____ "

   _____

UNIT 3 — CHANGE A VOWEL SOUND

WARM-UP ACTIVITY 1 REVIEW

Directions to Facilitator

Read the following items to students. Have them respond orally. When appropriate, pause to wait for students to respond.

1. Listen to this word: *trick.* Does *trick* end with a /g/ sound?

2. Say *bought.* Now say the three sounds in *bought.*

3. Say *bale.* Now say *bowl.* What sound was different in the second word?

4. Say /b/ /æ/ /g/. Blend those sounds together. Which word do they make?

5. Say *ride.* Now say *road.* What sound was different in the second word?

6. Look at the eight boldface Think It Through words in Warm-up Activity 1. Which word rhymes with *chimp*?

7. Say *bake.* What is the first sound in that word?

8. Say *rag.* What is the middle sound in that word?

CHANGE A VOWEL SOUND

WARM-UP ACTIVITY 2

THINK IT THROUGH

Directions: Change a vowel sound to make the word:

1. *will,* a word that means "a place where water can be found" _____

2. *trip,* a word that means "a device for capturing someone or something"
    _____

3. *dim,* a word that means "a structure for stopping the flow of water" _____

4. *foil,* a word that means "the opposite of succeed" _____

5. *blink,* a word that means "the way a piece of paper looks before it is written on"
    _____

6. *fare,* a word that means "a raging blaze" _____

7. *coat,* a word that means "a grown-up kitten" _____

8. *knit,* a word that means "an annoying, little insect" _____

WRITE A RIDDLE

Directions: Write your own riddle on the long line. Then, exchange riddles with a friend and have him or her write the answers on the short line below each clue. Change a vowel sound to make the word:

1. *tell,* a word that means " _____ "
    _____

2. *shook,* a word that means " _____ "
    _____

CHANGE A VOWEL SOUND

WARM-UP ACTIVITY 2 REVIEW

Directions to Facilitator

Read the following items to students. Have them respond orally. When appropriate, pause to wait for students to respond.

1. Look at the eight boldface Think It Through words in Warm-up Activity 2. Which word rhymes with *boil*?

2. Say /t/ /r/ /ɪ/ /p/. Blend those sounds together. Which word do they make?

3. Say *will*. Now say the three sounds in *will*.

4. Listen to this word: *blink.* Does *blink* begin with a /b/ sound?

5. Say /n/ /ɪ/ /t/. Blend those sounds together. Which word do they make?

6. Say *fare.* Now say *fire.* What sound was different in the second word?

7. Say *dim.* What is the middle sound in that word?

8. Say *coat.* What is the first sound in that word?

CHANGE A VOWEL SOUND

WARM-UP ACTIVITY 3

THINK IT THROUGH

Directions: Change a vowel sound to make the word:

1. **best,** a word that means "how to keep a turkey moist while it roasts"_____

2. **pill,** a word that means "something you can swim in"_____

3. **cheer,** a word that means "a job to be done" _____

4. **meat,** a word that means "an area around a castle that is filled with water"

   _____

5. **chose,** a word that means "a game in which you move pieces on a board to checkmate the opposing king" _____

6. **mouth,** a word that means "a flying insect known for making holes in clothing"

   _____

7. **man,** a word that means "to cry in pain" _____

8. **grain,** a word that means "the color of grass" _____

WRITE A RIDDLE

Directions: Write your own riddle on the long line. Then, exchange riddles with a friend and have him or her write the answers on the short line below each clue. Change a vowel sound to make the word:

1. **clown,** a word that means "_____"

   _____

2. **flat,** a word that means "_____"

   _____

CHANGE A VOWEL SOUND

WARM-UP ACTIVITY 3 REVIEW

Directions to Facilitator

Read the following items to students. Have them respond orally. When appropriate, pause to wait for students to respond.

1. Look at the eight boldface Think It Through words in Warm-up Activity 3. Which word rhymes with *sear*?

2. Say *meat.* Now say *moat.* What sound was different in the second word?

3. Say *pill.* Now say the three sounds in *pill.*

4. Say /ʧ/ /oʊ/ /z/. Blend those sounds together. Which word do they make?

5. Look at the eight boldface Think It Through words in Warm-up Activity 3. Which word rhymes with *south*?

6. Listen to this word: *best.* Does *best* end with a /s/ sound?

7. Say *grain.* What is the first sound in *grain*?

8. Say *man.* Now say the three sounds in *man.*

CHANGE A VOWEL SOUND

WARM-UP ACTIVITY 4

THINK IT THROUGH

Directions: Change a vowel sound to make the word:

1. **trap,** a word that means "a group of soldiers" _____

2. **vogue,** a word that means "not clearly defined, stated in indefinite terms"
   _____

3. **wind,** a word that means "a slender rod used by magicians" _____

4. **take,** a word that means "a small, short nail with a flat, broad head"
   _____

5. **space,** a word that means "a seasoning for foods" _____

6. **past,** a word that means "someone who is annoying" _____

7. **jelly,** a word that means "joyous, full of high spirits" _____

8. **time,** a word that means "not wild" _____

WRITE A RIDDLE

Directions: Write your own riddle on the long line. Then, exchange riddles with a friend and have him or her write the answers on the short line below each clue. Change a vowel sound to make the word:

1. **see,** a word that means "_____"
   _____

2. **feet,** a word that means "_____"
   _____

CHANGE A VOWEL SOUND

WARM-UP ACTIVITY 4 REVIEW

Directions to Facilitator

Read the following items to students. Have them respond orally. When appropriate, pause to wait for students to respond.

1. Say *space.* Now say the four sounds in *space.*

2. Listen to this word: *past.* Does *past* begin with a /p/?

3. Look at the eight boldface Think It Through words in Warm-up Activity 4. Which word rhymes with *rogue*?

4. Say *time.* What is the last sound in that word?

5. Say *jelly.* Now say *jolly.* What sound was different in the second word?

6. Say /t/ /r/ /æ/ /p/ Blend those sounds together. Which word do they make?

7. Say *take.* Now say *tack.* What sound was different in the second word?

8. Say *wind.* What is the first sound in that word?

PHONOLOGICAL HUMOR ACTIVITIES

FACILITATOR NOTES

The *Phonological Humor Activities* in this unit contain words with a vowel sound substituted to make the item into a joke. Students must change a vowel sound in the funny word to determine what the real word is. Because more than one letter can represent a single sound, students should focus on how words are pronounced rather than spelled.

Complete the examples below orally with the students. This will give them the opportunity to hear acceptable responses to the questions. Because the word with a vowel sound changed and the funny word always sound similar, this fact alone will not be a complete answer to question d. Students should rely on their own world knowledge of the subject to explain the relationship between the words.

An answer key is provided for the activities (see pages 136—137). The answers are only suggestions. The correctness of students' responses is left to the discretion of the facilitator.

EXAMPLE 1

Q: What sea creature has to have a good reason for doing something?

A: A porpoise.

a. Which word in the answer makes the joke funny? (*porpoise*)

b. What do you think the real word is? (*purpose*)

c. Which words or phrases give you a clue why the funny word was used? (*sea creature* and *reason*)

d. Explain why the funny word was used. (A reason is a purpose, which sounds like *porpoise*, and a porpoise is a sea creature.)

EXAMPLE 2

Q: What do you call a big group of boring, spotted dogs?

A: 101 Dullmatians.

a. Which word makes the joke funny? (*Dullmatians*)

b. What do you think the real word is? (*Dalmatians*)

c. Which words or phrases give you a clue why the funny word was used? (*big group, boring,* and *spotted dogs*)

d. Explain why the funny word was used. (*Dull* is another word for *boring,* and Dalmatians have spots and were in a book and movie called *101 Dalmatians.*)

UNIT 3

CHANGE A VOWEL SOUND

PHONOLOGICAL HUMOR ACTIVITY 1

Directions: Answer the questions below each item.

1. **Q: What do baby birds call their parents?**
   A: Mother and Feather.

   a. Which word in the answer makes the joke funny? _____

   b. What do you think the real word is? _____

   c. Which words or phrases give you a clue why the funny word was used? _____

   d. Explain why the funny word was used. _____

   _____

2. **Q: What is the difference between shillings and pence?**
   A: You can walk down the street without shillings, but you can't walk down the street without pence.

   a. Which word in the answer makes the joke funny? _____

   b. What do you think the real word is? _____

   c. Which words or phrases give you a clue why the funny word was used? _____

   d. Explain why the funny word was used. _____

   _____

3. **Q: What is a sick relative of a crocodile?**
   A: An illigator.

   a. Which word makes the joke funny? _____

   b. What do you think the real word is? _____

   c. Which words or phrases give you a clue why the funny word was used? _____

   d. Explain why the funny word was used. _____

   _____

CHANGE A VOWEL SOUND

PHONOLOGICAL HUMOR ACTIVITY 2

Directions: Answer the questions below each item.

1. **Q: When do ghosts have to stop scaring people?**

   A: When they lose their haunting license.

   a.   Which word in the answer makes the joke funny? _____

   b.   What do you think the real word is? _____

   c.   Which words or phrases give you a clue why the funny word was used? _____

   d.   Explain why the funny word was used. _____

   _____

2. **Q: Why are Egyptian children so good?**

   A: Because they respect their mummies.

   a.   Which word in the answer makes the joke funny? _____

   b.   What do you think the real word is? _____

   c.   Which words or phrases give you a clue why the funny word was used? _____

   d.   Explain why the funny word was used. _____

   _____

3. **Phoning a bee is so annoying; you always get a buzzy signal.**

   a.   Which word in the sentence makes the joke funny?_____

   b.   What do you think the real word is? _____

   c.   Which words or phrases give you a clue why the funny word was used? _____

   d.   Explain why the funny word was used. _____

   _____

UNIT 3

CHANGE A VOWEL SOUND

PHONOLOGICAL HUMOR ACTIVITY 3

Directions: Answer the questions below each item.

1. **Q: What do you get if you cross a clock and a chicken?**
   A: An alarm cluck.

   a. Which word in the answer makes the joke funny? _____

   b. What do you think the real word is? _____

   c. Which words or phrases give you a clue why the funny word was used? _____

   d. Explain why the funny word was used. _____

   _____

2. **Q: What do you give to an elk with indigestion?**
   A: Elka-Seltzer.

   a. Which word makes the joke funny? _____

   b. What do you think the real word is? _____

   c. Which words or phrases give you a clue why the funny word was used? _____

   d. Explain why the funny word was used. _____

   _____

3. **Q: Did you hear about the acrobat at the circus?**
   A: He always had a chap on his shoulder.

   a. Which word in the answer makes the joke funny? _____

   b. What do you think the real word is? _____

   c. Which words or phrases give you a clue why the funny word was used? _____

   d. Explain why the funny word was used. _____

   _____

CHANGE A VOWEL SOUND

PHONOLOGICAL HUMOR ACTIVITY 4

Directions: Answer the questions below each item.

1. **Q: Why doesn't a frog jump when it is sad?**
   A: It's too unhoppy.

   a. Which word in the answer makes the joke funny? _____

   b. What do you think the real word is? _____

   c. Which words or phrases give you a clue why the funny word was used? _____

   d. Explain why the funny word was used. _____

   _____

2. **A man came home from work dripping wet. "Oh dear, it's raining cats and dogs," said his wife. "I know," the man replied. "I just stepped in a poodle."**

   a. Which word in the man's reply makes the joke funny? _____

   b. What do you think the real word is? _____

   c. Which words or phrases give you a clue why the funny word was used? _____

   d. Explain why the funny word was used. _____

   _____

3. **Q: What does Tarzan sing at Christmastime?**
   A: "Jungle Bells."

   a. Which word in the answer makes the joke funny? _____

   b. What do you think the real word is? _____

   c. Which words or phrases give you a clue why the funny word was used? _____

   d. Explain why the funny word was used. _____

   _____

Sounds Like Fun: Activities for Developing Phonological Awareness, Revised Edition
Copyright © 2009 by Cecile Cyrul Spector. All rights reserved.

UNIT 3

CHANGE A VOWEL SOUND

PHONOLOGICAL HUMOR ACTIVITIES

REVIEW AND REFLECTION

1. a. Look through the Phonological Humor Activities you have just finished. Which joke was the easiest for you to understand?

_____

   b. Why do you think it was the easiest?

_____

_____

2. a. Which joke was the hardest for you to understand?

_____

   b. Why do you think it was the hardest?

_____

_____

3. a. Which joke did you think was the funniest?

_____

   b. Why do you think it was the funniest?

_____

_____

4. The activities in this unit are based on changing a vowel sound. Describe some jobs people have that require them to think about how vowel sounds can be changed. (Hint: Think about people who write or sing for a living.)

_____

_____

5. How does knowing about sounds in words help you when you are reading or spelling?

_____

_____

_____

UNIT 4

ADD A
CONSONANT SOUND

WARM-UP ACTIVITIES

FACILITATOR NOTES

Using the first two *Warm-up Activities* in this unit, students practice adding a consonant sound to a word beginning or ending with a vowel sound. Using the second two Warm-up Activities, students practice adding a consonant sound to a word beginning or ending with a consonant sound to work on forming consonant clusters. Through these processes, students make new words that fit the given definitions. The Warm-up Activities are provided to prepare students for the *Phonological Humor Activities* on pages 81–85.

Using the *Think It Through* activities, students solve a puzzle. They use their world knowledge to determine the word that is appropriate for a given definition. Because more than one letter can represent a single sound (e.g., /n/ in kneel), students should focus on how words are pronounced rather than spelled. If desired, compare students' responses with those in the answer key (see page 137).

The *Write a Riddle* activities give students a chance to create some riddles of their own. Students think of a consonant sound to add to the boldface word to make it into a different word. Then, they write their own clue so that someone else can solve the riddle. Encourage students to swap their Write a Riddle activities to solve each others' riddles.

A review page follows each warm-up page. The purpose of the review activities is to provide additional phonological awareness practice. Using the boldface words from the preceding Warm-Up Activity, students find rhyming words; match sounds to words; segment words; and identify, manipulate, and blend sounds. The review activities should be conducted orally.

Complete the following examples orally with the students. This will give them the opportunity to practice the two types of Warm-up Activities before trying some activities on their own. Provide as much or as little support as necessary for the activities.

THINK IT THROUGH

Directions: Add a consonant sound to make the word:

1. *too,* a word that means "the sound a horn makes" (*toot*)

2. *top,* a word that means "the opposite of go" (*stop*)

WRITE A RIDDLE

Directions: Add a consonant sound to make the word:

1. *it,* a word that means "_____"

    Example answer: "the stone in the center of a peach" (*pit*)

2. *par,* a word that means "_____"

    Example answer: "an area with trees and flowers used for recreation" (*park*)

UNIT 4

ADD A CONSONANT SOUND

WARM-UP ACTIVITY 1

THINK IT THROUGH

Directions: Add a consonant sound to make the word:

1. **too,** a word that means "a place where you can get a cavity" _____

2. **hi,** a word that means "a home for honeybees" _____

3. **guy,** a word that means "to show the way" _____

4. **say,** a word that means "to rescue" _____

5. **sigh,** a word that means "to write your name at the end of a letter"
_____

6. **ape,** a word that means "a piece of clothing that Superman wears"
_____

7. **up,** a word that means "a young dog" _____

8. **oat,** a word that means "a seagoing vessel" _____

WRITE A RIDDLE

Directions: Write your own riddle on the long line. Then, exchange riddles with a friend and have him or her write the answers on the short line below each clue. Add a consonant sound to make the word:

1. **an,** a word that means " _____ "
_____

2. **ate,** a word that means " _____ "
_____

Sounds Like Fun: Activities for Developing Phonological Awareness, Revised Edition
Copyright © 2009 by Cecile Cyrul Spector. All rights reserved.

ADD A CONSONANT SOUND

WARM-UP ACTIVITY 1 REVIEW

Directions to Facilitator

Read the following items to students. Have them respond orally. When appropriate, pause to wait for students to respond.

1. Say *ape.* What is the last sound in that word?

2. Say /s/ /aɪ/. Blend those sounds together. Which word do they make?

3. Listen to this word: *up.* Does *up* end with a /p/ sound?

4. Say *too.* What is the first sound in that word?

5. Look at the eight boldface Think It Through words in Warm-up Activity 1. Which word rhymes with *weigh*?

6. Say *oat.* What is the last sound in that word?

7. Listen to this word: *guy.* Does *guy* start with a /k/ sound?

8. Say *hi.* Now say *hive.* What sound was added in the second word?

ADD A CONSONANT SOUND

WARM-UP ACTIVITY 2

THINK IT THROUGH

Directions: Add a consonant sound to make the word:

1. *ore,* a word that means "the way you feel when you overdo exercise" _____

2. *owl,* a word that means "the sound a wolf makes" _____

3. *wee,* a word that means "something you pull out of a garden" _____

4. *may,* a word that means "the long, heavy fur that grows around a lion's neck"
   _____

5. *eel,* a word that means "the covering of a banana" _____

6. *end,* a word that means "to stoop to touch your toes" _____

7. *ill,* a word that means "a kind of pickle" _____

8. *ink,* a word that means "a place where people go to skate" _____

WRITE A RIDDLE

Directions: Write your own riddle on the long line. Then, exchange riddles with a friend and have him or her write the answers on the short line below each clue. Add a consonant sound to make the word:

1. *at,* a word that means " _____ "
   _____

2. *ail,* a word that means " _____ "
   _____

ADD A CONSONANT SOUND

WARM-UP ACTIVITY 2 REVIEW

Directions to Facilitator

Read the following items to students. Have them respond orally. When appropriate, pause to wait for students to respond.

1. Say *ink.* What is the last sound in that word?

2. Say *eel.* What is the last sound in that word?

3. Look at the eight boldface Think It Through words in Warm-up Activity 2. Which word rhymes with *jowl*?

4. Say /m/ /eɪ/. Blend those sounds together. Which word do they make?

5. Say *ill.* Now say the two sounds in that word.

6. Say *ore.* Now say *sore.* What sound was added in the second word?

7. Say /ɛ/ /n/ /d/. Blend those sounds together. Which word do they make?

8. Listen to this word: *wee.* Does *wee* start with /r/?

UNIT 4

ADD A CONSONANT SOUND

WARM-UP ACTIVITY 3

THINK IT THROUGH

Directions: Add a consonant sound to make the word:

1. *lush,* a word that means "partially melted or watery snow" _____

2. *fail,* a word that means "weak and delicate" _____

3. *bag,* a word that means "to boast" _____

4. *rank,* a word that means "a trick or practical joke" _____

5. *gas,* a word that means "a sudden intake of breath" _____

6. *tin,* a word that means "to add a little bit of color"_____

7. *char,* a word that means "a compelling attractiveness" _____

8. *rave,* a word that means "fearless in the face of danger" _____

WRITE A RIDDLE

Directions: Write your own riddle on the long line. Then, exchange riddles with a friend and have him or her write the answers on the short line below each clue. Add a consonant sound to make the word:

1. *sole,* a word that means " _____ "

_____

2. *rain,* a word that means " _____ "

_____

ADD A CONSONANT SOUND

WARM-UP ACTIVITY 3 REVIEW

Directions to Facilitator

Read the following items to students. Have them respond orally. When appropriate, pause to wait for students to respond.

1. Say /g/ /æ/ /s/. Blend those sounds together. Which word do they make?

2. Say *char.* What is the first sound in that word?

3. Listen to this word: *rank.* Does *rank* end with /k/?

4. Say *fail.* Now say *frail.* What sound was added in the second word?

5. Say /l/ /ʌ/ /ʃ/. Blend those sounds together. Which word do they make?

6. Say *bowl.* Now say the three sounds in that word.

7. Look at the eight boldface Think It Through words in Warm-up Activity 3. Which word rhymes with *lag*?

8. Say *tin.* Now say *tint.* What sound was added in the second word?

ADD A CONSONANT SOUND

WARM-UP ACTIVITY 4

THINK IT THROUGH

Directions: Add a consonant sound to make the word:

1. *rip,* a word that means "to have a strong hold on something" _____

2. *law,* a word that means "a defect or imperfection" _____

3. *ten,* a word that means "to care for or watch over" _____

4. *sale,* a word that means "not fresh"_____

5. *rust,* a word that means "to have faith in someone"_____

6. *old,* a word that means "to give a desired shape" _____

7. *seam,* a word that means "the vapor that rises when water boils" _____

8. *rope,* a word that means "to reach for something blindly or uncertainly"
   _____

WRITE A RIDDLE

Directions: Write your own riddle on the long line. Then, exchange riddles with a friend and have him or her write the answers on the short line below each clue. Add a consonant sound to make the word:

1. *bead,* a word that means " _____ "
   _____

2. *lap,* a word that means "_____ "
   _____

ADD A CONSONANT SOUND

WARM-UP ACTIVITY 4 REVIEW

Directions to Facilitator

Read the following items to students. Have them respond orally. When appropriate, pause to wait for students to respond.

1. Say *mole.* Now say *mold.* What sound was added in the second word?

2. Say *rope.* What is the last sound in that word?

3. Say /r/ /ʌ/ /s/ /t/. Blend those sounds together. Which word do they make?

4. Listen to this word: *ten.* Does *ten* start with /d/?

5. Say /s/ /i/ /m/. Blend those sounds together. Which word do they make?

6. Say *law.* What is the first sound in that word?

7. Listen to this word: *rip.* Does *rip* end with /b/?

8. Look at the eight boldface Think It Through words in Warm-up Activity 4. Which word rhymes with *bale*?

PHONOLOGICAL HUMOR ACTIVITIES

FACILITATOR NOTES

The *Phonological Humor Activities* in this unit contain words with a consonant sound deleted to make the item into a joke. Students must add a consonant sound to the funny word to determine what the real word is. Because more than one letter can represent a single sound, students should focus on how words are pronounced rather than spelled.

Complete the examples below orally with the students. This will give them the opportunity to hear acceptable responses to the questions. Because the word with a consonant sound taken away and the funny word always sound similar, this fact alone will not be a complete answer to question d. Students should rely on their own world knowledge of the subject to explain the relationship between the words.

An answer key is provided for the activities (see page 138). The answers are only suggestions. The correctness of students' responses is left to the discretion of the facilitator.

EXAMPLE 1

Q: What kind of jeans do ghosts wear?

A: Boo jeans.

a.   Which word in the answer makes the joke funny? (*boo*)

b.   What do you think the real word is? (*blue*)

c.   Which words or phrases give you a clue why the funny word was used? (*ghosts* and *jeans*)

d.   Explain why the funny word was used. (Ghosts say "boo," which sounds like *blue;* and people wear blue jeans, so ghosts would wear boo jeans.)

EXAMPLE 2

Artificial snow is made of snowfakes.

a.   Which word in the sentence makes the joke funny? (*snowfakes*)

b.   What do you think the real word is? (*snowflakes*)

c.   Which words or phrases give you a clue why the funny word was used? (*artificial* and *snow*)

d.   Explain why the funny word was used. (*Fake,* which sounds like *flake,* is another way of saying *artificial;* and snow comes down in flakes.)

UNIT 4

ADD A CONSONANT SOUND

PHONOLOGICAL HUMOR ACTIVITY 1

Directions: Answer the questions below each item.

1. **Q: What musical instrument does a frog play?**

    A: The hopsichord.

    a.   Which word makes the joke funny?_____

    b.   What do you think the real word is? _____

    c.   Which words or phrases give you a clue why the funny word was used? _____

    d.   Explain why the funny word was used. _____

    _____

2. **When Randy tried out for the swimming team, he swam very badly. The coach told him, "Between you and me, Randy, you sink!"**

    a.   Which word in the coach's statement makes the joke funny? _____

    b.   What do you think the real word is? _____

    c.   Which words or phrases give you a clue why the funny word was used? _____

    d.   Explain why the funny word was used. _____

    _____

3. **Q: Why did the secret agent take two aspirins and go to bed?**

    A: He had a head code.

    a.   Which word in the answer makes the joke funny? _____

    b.   What do you think the real word is? _____

    c.   Which words or phrases give you a clue why the funny word was used? _____

    d.   Explain why the funny word was used. _____

    _____

UNIT 4

ADD A CONSONANT SOUND

PHONOLOGICAL HUMOR ACTIVITY 2

Directions: Answer the questions below each item.

1. **Q: What is a cow's favorite fruit?**

   A: Catteloupe.

   a.   Which word makes the joke funny? _____

   b.   What do you think the real word is? _____

   c.   Which words or phrases give you a clue why the funny word was used? _____

   d.   Explain why the funny word was used.   _____

   _____

2. **Ellen: My husband's name is Ed. If I have a son, should I name him Ed also?**
   Sabrina: Sure. Everyone knows two Eds are better than one.

   a.   Which word in Sabrina's answer makes the joke funny? _____

   b.   What do you think the real word is? _____

   c.   Which words or phrases give you a clue why the funny word was used? _____

   d.   Explain why the funny word was used.   _____

   _____

3. **After the game, the showers were filled with team.**

   a.   Which word in the sentence makes the joke funny? _____

   b.   What do you think the real word is? _____

   c.   Which words or phrases give you a clue why the funny word was used? _____

   d.   Explain why the funny word was used.   _____

   _____

> UNIT 4

ADD A CONSONANT SOUND

PHONOLOGICAL HUMOR ACTIVITY 3

Directions: Answer the questions below each item.

1. **Q: What can be used to gather information on all of the monkeys in a zoo?**
   A: An ape recorder.

   a. Which word in the answer makes the joke funny? _____

   b. What do you think the real word is? _____

   c. Which words or phrases give you a clue why the funny word was used? _____

   d. Explain why the funny word was used. _____

   _____

2. **Q: What do cowboys call a doctor's hypodermic needle?**
   A: A sick shooter.

   a. Which word makes the joke funny? _____

   b. What do you think the real word is? _____

   c. Which words or phrases give you a clue why the funny word was used? _____

   d. Explain why the funny word was used. _____

   _____

3. **Q: Which president had trouble with the dog catcher?**
   A: Rover Cleveland.

   a. Which word in the answer makes the joke funny? _____

   b. What do you think the real word is? _____

   c. Which words or phrases give you a clue why the funny word was used? _____

   d. Explain why the funny word was used. _____

   _____

UNIT 4

ADD A CONSONANT SOUND

PHONOLOGICAL HUMOR ACTIVITY 4

Directions: Answer the questions below each item.

1. **Q: What is a ghost's favorite dessert?**
    A: Booberry pie.

    a. Which word in the answer makes the joke funny? _____

    b. What do you think the real word is? _____

    c. Which words or phrases give you a clue why the funny word was used? _____

    d. Explain why the funny word was used. _____

    _____

2. **Q: What do you get if you cross a movie house and a swimming pool?**
    A: A dive-in theater.

    a. Which word in the answer makes the joke funny? _____

    b. What do you think the real word is? _____

    c. Which words or phrases give you a clue why the funny word was used? _____

    d. Explain why the funny word was used. _____

    _____

3. **Q: How do you top a car?**
    A: You tep on the brake.

    a. Which words make the joke funny? _____

    b. What do you think the real words are? _____

    c. Which words or phrases give you a clue why the funny words were used? _____

    d. Explain why the funny words were used. _____

    _____

UNIT 4

ADD A CONSONANT SOUND

PHONOLOGICAL HUMOR ACTIVITIES

REVIEW AND REFLECTION

1. a. Look through the Phonological Humor Activities you have just finished. Which joke was the easiest for you to understand?

    _____

    b. Why do you think it was the easiest?

    _____

    _____

2. a. Which joke was the hardest for you to understand?

    _____

    b. Why do you think it was the hardest?

    _____

    _____

3. a. Which joke did you think was the funniest?

    _____

    b. Why do you think it was the funniest?

    _____

    _____

4. The activities in this unit are based on adding a consonant sound. When else have you seen a consonant sound added to a word? (Hint: Think of some word games you have played.)

    _____

    _____

5. How does knowing about sounds in words help people at work? (Hint: Think about people who get paid to work with words.)

    _____

    _____

    _____

UNIT 5

CHALLENGE ACTIVITIES

CHALLENGE ACTIVITIES

FACILITATOR NOTES

The *Challenge Activities* in this unit contain jokes that have more than one sound change. For example, a word in this joke has both a sound added and a sound changed:

Q: What do you call two pigs fighting?
A: Ham-to-ham combat.

The word *ham* could be *hand,* as in hand-to-hand combat. To make *ham* into *hand,* /d/ is added and /m/ is changed to /n/. When sound changes are made, spelling changes are likely to occur. For this reason, students should focus on how words are pronounced rather than spelled.

Complete the examples below orally with the students. This will give them the opportunity to hear acceptable responses to the questions. Because the word with sound changes and the funny word always sound similar, this fact alone will not be a complete answer to question d. Students should rely on their own world knowledge of the subject to explain the relationship between the words.

An answer key is provided for the activities (see pages 139–141). The answers are only suggestions. The correctness of students' responses is left to the discretion of the facilitator.

EXAMPLE 1

Q: What is round, purple, and orbits the sun?
A: Planet of the Grapes.

a.   Which word in the answer makes the joke funny? (*grapes*)

b.   What do you think the real word is? (*apes*)

c.   Which words or phrases give you a clue why the funny word was used? (*round, purple,* and *orbits the sun*)

d.   Explain why the funny word was used. (Planets orbit the sun, and some grapes are round and purple. *Planet of the Grapes* sounds like the movie title *Planet of the Apes.*)

EXAMPLE 2

Q: What is in the beginning of a geography book?
A: The table of continents.

a.   Which word makes the joke funny? (*continents*)

b.   What do you think the real word is? (*contents*)

c.   Which words or phrases give you a clue why the funny word was used? (*beginning* and *geography book*)

d.   Explain why the funny word was used. (The table of contents is found in the front matter of a book, and geography is a subject that studies land masses such as continents.)

> UNIT 5

CHALLENGE ACTIVITIES

CHALLENGE ACTIVITY 1

Directions: Answer the questions below each item.

1. **Q: What injury are Olympic athletes likely to suffer?**
   A: A slipped discus.

   a. Which word in the answer makes the joke funny? _____

   b. What do you think the real word is? _____

   c. Which words or phrases give you a clue why the funny word was used? _____

   d. Explain why the funny word was used. _____

   _____

2. **Q: How are all sheep alike?**
   A: They have mutton in common.

   a. Which word in the answer makes the joke funny? _____

   b. What do you think the real word is? _____

   c. Which words or phrases give you a clue why the funny word was used? _____

   d. Explain why the funny word was used. _____

   _____

3. **Q: Who lives in the ocean, has tentacles, and is quick on the draw?**
   A: Billy the Squid.

   a. Which word in the answer makes the joke funny? _____

   b. What do you think the real word is? _____

   c. Which words or phrases give you a clue why the funny word was used? _____

   d. Explain why the funny word was used. _____

   _____

UNIT 5 — CHALLENGE ACTIVITIES

CHALLENGE ACTIVITY 2

Directions: Answer the questions below each item.

1. **Q: What is green and sings?**
   A: Elvis Parsley.

   a. Which word in the answer makes the joke funny? _____

   b. What do you think the real word is? _____

   c. Which words or phrases give you a clue why the funny word was used? _____

   d. Explain why the funny word was used. _____

   _____

2. **Q: How do you catch a unique rabbit?**   **A: You 'neak up on it.**
   Q: How do you catch a tame rabbit?   **A: The tame way.**

   a. Which words in the answers make the joke funny? _____

   b. What do you think the real words are? _____

   c. Which words or phrases give you a clue why the funny words were used? _____

   d. Explain why the funny words were used. _____

   _____

3. **Q: Who was Sleeping Beauty's sad sister?**
   A: Weeping Beauty.

   a. Which word in the answer makes the joke funny? _____

   b. What do you think the real word is? _____

   c. Which words or phrases give you a clue why the funny word was used? _____

   d. Explain why the funny word was used. _____

   _____

CHALLENGE ACTIVITIES

CHALLENGE ACTIVITY 3

Directions: Answer the questions below each item.

1. **Q: Why should you never insult an alien?**

   A: It might get its feelers hurt.

   a. Which word in the answer makes the joke funny? _____

   b. What do you think the real word is? _____

   c. Which words or phrases give you a clue why the funny word was used? _____

   d. Explain why the funny word was used. _____

   _____

2. **Q: What do you call a vending machine that doesn't return your money?**

   A: Coinivorous.

   a. Which word makes the joke funny? _____

   b. What do you think the real word is? _____

   c. Which words or phrases give you a clue why the funny word was used? _____

   d. Explain why the funny word was used. _____

   _____

3. **Q: What did the sign read on the window in Shakespeare's restaurant?**

   A: "What foods these morsels be."

   a. Which words in the answer make the joke funny? _____

   b. What do you think the real words are? _____

   c. Which words or phrases give you a clue why the funny words were used? _____

   d. Explain why the funny words were used. _____

   _____

CHALLENGE ACTIVITIES

CHALLENGE ACTIVITY 4

Directions: Answer the questions below each item.

1. **Q: What kind of birthday parties do lambs like?**
   A: Sheepovers.

   a.   Which word makes the joke funny? _____

   b.   What do you think the real word is? _____

   c.   Which words or phrases give you a clue why the funny word was used? _____

   d.   Explain why the funny word was used. _____

   _____

2. **Q: What is the secret to successful dieting?**
   A: The triumph of mind over platter.

   a.   Which word in the answer makes the joke funny? _____

   b.   What do you think the real word is? _____

   c.   Which words or phrases give you a clue why the funny word was used? _____

   d.   Explain why the funny word was used. _____

   _____

3. **Q: What kind of glasses does James Bond wear?**
   A: Spyfocals.

   a.   Which word makes the joke funny?_____

   b.   What do you think the real word is? _____

   c.   Which words or phrases give you a clue why the funny word was used? _____

   d.   Explain why the funny word was used. _____

   _____

> UNIT 5

> CHALLENGE ACTIVITIES

CHALLENGE ACTIVITY 5

Directions: Answer the questions below each item.

1. **Q: Where do you send a sick pony?**
   A: To the horsepital.

   a. Which word makes the joke funny?_____

   b. What do you think the real word is? _____

   c. Which words or phrases give you a clue why the funny word was used? _____

   d. Explain why the funny word was used. _____

   _____

2. **Q: What does Dracula do when he has a cold?**
   A: He's always coffin.

   a. Which word in the answer makes the joke funny? _____

   b. What do you think the real word is? _____

   c. Which words or phrases give you a clue why the funny word was used? _____

   d. Explain why the funny word was used. _____

   _____

3. **Q: What did the woman say when the doctor asked if she had been sick?**
   A: "Of cough!"

   a. Which word makes the joke funny?_____

   b. What do you think the real word is? _____

   c. Which words or phrases give you a clue why the funny word was used? _____

   d. Explain why the funny word was used. _____

   _____

UNIT 5

CHALLENGE ACTIVITIES

CHALLENGE ACTIVITY 6

Directions: Answer the questions below each item.

1. **Q: Where do seagulls like to hang out?**
   A: Where the buoys are.

   a. Which word in the answer makes the joke funny? _____

   b. What do you think the real word is? _____

   c. Which words or phrases give you a clue why the funny word was used? _____

   d. Explain why the funny word was used. _____

   _____

2. **Q: What happened to the nuclear scientist who swallowed a uranium pill?**
   A: He got atomic ache.

   a. Which word in the answer makes the joke funny? _____

   b. What do you think the real words are? _____

   c. Which words or phrases give you a clue why the funny word was used? _____

   d. Explain why the funny word was used. _____

   _____

3. **Q: Why did the pirate put a chicken where he buried his treasure?**
   A: Because eggs marks the spot.

   a. Which word in the answer makes the joke funny? _____

   b. What do you think the real word is? _____

   c. Which words or phrases give you a clue why the funny word was used? _____

   d. Explain why the funny word was used. _____

   _____

CHALLENGE ACTIVITY 7

Directions: Answer the questions below each item.

1. **Q: What did the judge say to the dentist?**
   A: "I want you to pull the tooth, the whole tooth, and nothing but the tooth."

   a. Which word in the answer makes the joke funny? _____

   b. What do you think the real word is? _____

   c. Which words or phrases give you a clue why the funny word was used? _____

   d. Explain why the funny word was used. _____

   _____

2. **Q: What happened when the new attendant met the pilot?**
   A: It was love at first flight.

   a. Which word in the answer makes the joke funny? _____

   b. What do you think the real word is? _____

   c. Which words or phrases give you a clue why the funny word was used? _____

   d. Explain why the funny word was used. _____

   _____

3. **Q: What would you get if Batman and Robin were stampeded by elephants?**
   A: Flatman and Ribbon.

   a. Which words in the answer make the joke funny? _____

   b. What do you think the real words are? _____

   c. Which words or phrases give you a clue why the funny words were used?_____

   d. Explain why the funny words were used. _____

   _____

UNIT 5

CHALLENGE ACTIVITIES

CHALLENGE ACTIVITY 8

Directions: Answer the questions below each item.

1. **Q: Why is the baseball championship not a laughing matter?**
   A: Because it's the World Serious.

   a. Which word in the answer makes the joke funny? _____

   b. What do you think the real word is? _____

   c. Which words or phrases give you a clue why the funny word was used? _____

   d. Explain why the funny word was used. _____

   _____

2. **Q: What did the loud mouse say to the quiet mouse?**
   A: Squeak up!

   a. Which word in the answer makes the joke funny? _____

   b. What do you think the real word is? _____

   c. Which words or phrases give you a clue why the funny word was used? _____

   d. Explain why the funny word was used. _____

   _____

3. **Q: What is the most dangerous light?**
   A: Ultraviolent.

   a. Which word makes the joke funny?_____

   b. What do you think the real word is? _____

   c. Which words or phrases give you a clue why the funny word was used? _____

   d. Explain why the funny word was used. _____

   _____

CHALLENGE ACTIVITY 9

Directions: Answer the questions below each item.

1. **Q: What do mice wear to school on gym days?**
   A: Squeakers.

   a. Which word makes the joke funny? _____

   b. What do you think the real word is? _____

   c. Which words or phrases give you a clue why the funny word was used? _____

   d. Explain why the funny word was used. _____

   _____

2. **Q: Why do demons and ghouls get along so well?**
   A: Because demons are a ghoul's best friend.

   a. Which words in the answer make the joke funny? _____

   b. What do you think the real words are? _____

   c. Which words or phrases give you a clue why the funny words were used?_____

   d. Explain why the funny words were used. _____

   _____

3. **Q: What kind of medicine do you give to a sick elephant?**
   A: Peanutcillin.

   a. Which word makes the joke funny?_____

   b. What do you think the real word is? _____

   c. Which words or phrases give you a clue why the funny word was used? _____

   d. Explain why the funny word was used. _____

   _____

CHALLENGE ACTIVITY 10

Directions: Answer the questions below each item.

1. **Q: Which bear never grew up?**

    A: Peter Panda.

    a. Which word in the answer makes the joke funny? _____

    b. What do you think the real word is? _____

    c. Which words or phrases give you a clue why the funny word was used? _____

    d. Explain why the funny word was used. _____

    _____

2. **Q: What do you get when you cross a galaxy with a toad?**

    A: Star warts.

    a. Which word in the answer makes the joke funny? _____

    b. What do you think the real word is? _____

    c. Which words or phrases give you a clue why the funny word was used? _____

    d. Explain why the funny word was used. _____

    _____

3. **Jeff: I just had my appendix removed.**

    Andy: Have a scar?

    Jeff: No thanks, I don't smoke.

    a. Which word in Andy's question makes the joke funny? _____

    b. What do you think the real word is? _____

    c. Which words or phrases give you a clue why the funny word was used? _____

    d. Explain why the funny word was used. _____

    _____

CHALLENGE ACTIVITIES

CHALLENGE ACTIVITY 11

Directions: Answer the questions below each item.

1. **Q: What is Count Dracula's favorite snack?**
    A: Fangfurters.

    a. Which word makes the joke funny? _____

    b. What do you think the real word is? _____

    c. Which words or phrases give you a clue why the funny word was used? _____

    d. Explain why the funny word was used. _____

    _____

2. **Q: What did the auto mechanic say to his supervisor?**
    A: "Save the last dents for me."

    a. Which word in the answer makes the joke funny? _____

    b. What do you think the real word is? _____

    c. Which words or phrases give you a clue why the funny word was used? _____

    d. Explain why the funny word was used. _____

    _____

3. **Q: Where do ghosts like to eat lunch?**
    A: Pizza Haunt.

    a. Which word in the answer makes the joke funny? _____

    b. What do you think the real word is? _____

    c. Which words or phrases give you a clue why the funny word was used? _____

    d. Explain why the funny word was used. _____

    _____

UNIT 5

CHALLENGE ACTIVITIES

REVIEW AND REFLECTION

1. a. Which joke was the most challenging?

    _____

    b. Why do you think it was the most challenging?

    _____

    _____

2. What strategies help you when you don't understand a joke the first time you hear it?

    _____

    _____

3. How can knowing about sounds in words help you understand jokes and riddles?

    _____

    _____

4. How does the ability to understand humor help you in school?

    _____

    _____

5. How does the ability to understand humor help you at home and while with your friends?

    _____

    _____

    _____

UNIT 6

ADDITIONAL ACTIVITIES

ADDITIONAL ACTIVITIES

FACILITATOR NOTES

The *Additional Activities* in this unit offer a variety of ways to explore sound changes within a single word. Because a single sound can be represented by more than one letter, students should focus on how words are pronounced rather than spelled.

The items in this unit may be too difficult for 8- or 9-year-old students, or students with impaired language-learning skills. Have students try a few of the items, then decide whether to continue. If students appear frustrated or have considerable difficulty finding the appropriate response, discontinue the activity. Refer to the section titled Activities to Enhance Phonological Awareness on pages xxi–xxii before continuing with difficult activities.

The activities in this unit include some challenging items that explore the addition, deletion, or substitution of a sound within a word. The addition and deletion items, because they have the support of rhyming in the responses (e.g., "Add two sounds to the word *in* to make a word that means to twirl about rapidly" [*spin*]), are not as difficult as the items that deal with substituting a sound. Changing a sound offers a more extensive range of possibilities for the responses. For example, in the item "Change two sounds in the word *chimp* to make a word that means "an object that produces light," the word *chimp* needs to have a consonant change (/ʧ/ to /l/) and a vowel change (/ɪ/ to /æ/) to make the word *lamp*. Consequently, greater verbal mediation may be needed for these items.

Students may succeed with some activities in this unit and not others. Activities do not need to be done in the order in which they appear. For example, this unit ends with knock-knock jokes, placed in this unit because they lack the contextual cues present in the other jokes and riddles in this book. This lack of context may make the knock-knock jokes more difficult for some students. However, many students have been exposed to knock-knock jokes and can, with mediation, develop a strategy for understanding them.

Facilitators are urged to browse through the Additional Activities that follow and select those that match the students' needs. Many activities could have additional practice items developed with minimal effort. For example, the first activity is Take Away a Sound. Facilitators can easily provide more words beyond the three given if such practice is deemed necessary and appropriate.

An answer key is provided for the activities (see pages 142–144). The answers are only suggestions, and they do not include the full range of possibilities for activities like Take Away One or More Sounds (see page 106) or Words with Three Sounds (see page 117). The correctness of students' responses is left to the discretion of the facilitator.

In addition to those found in Sounds like Fun, many fun activities exist for exploring sound changes (e.g., poetry that depends on rhyming sound play, such as the poems found in Shel Silverstein's books). Anagrams also explore sound changes, as students rearrange the letters in words to make new words or phrases. Other activities include playing word games such as Hangman or The Name Game. Most of all, remember to have fun!

ADDITIONAL ACTIVITIES

TAKE AWAY ONE OR MORE SOUNDS

See how many words you can make by taking away one or more sounds—not letters—from the word **splatter.**

_____   _____

_____   _____

_____   _____

Next, see how many words you can make by taking away one or more sounds—not letters—from the word **strange.**

_____   _____

_____   _____

_____   _____

Finally, see how many words you can make by taking away one or more sounds—not letters—from the word **sprint.**

_____   _____

_____   _____

_____   _____

ADDITIONAL ACTIVITIES

TAKE AWAY A SOUND, THEN TWO

Activity 1

1. a.   Take away a sound from the word *flash* to make a word that means "to strike with a whip."
      _____

    b.   Take away two sounds from the word *flash* to make a word that means "a type of tree."
      _____

2. a.   Take away a sound from the word *stalk* to make a word that means "to speak."
      _____

    b.   Take away two sounds from the word *stalk* to make a word that means "a black-and-white diving sea bird."
      _____

3. a.   Take away a sound from the word **spark** to make a word that means "to place one's car in the lot of a shopping center."
      _____

    b.   Take away two sounds from the word **spark** to make a word that means "the standard score for each hole of a golf course."
      _____

4. a.   Take away a sound from the word **strip** to make a word that means "to fall over something."
      _____

    b.   Take away two sounds from the word **strip** to make a word that means "to tear apart."
      _____

Your Turn!

Directions: Select a word. Take away a sound—then two—to make new words.

Key Word	One Sound Taken Away	Two Sounds Taken Away
_____	_____	_____

ADDITIONAL ACTIVITIES

TAKE AWAY A SOUND, THEN TWO

Activity 2

1. a. Take away a sound from the word **braid** to make a word that means "a surprise attack."
   _____

   b. Take away two sounds from the word **braid** to make a word that means "to help."
   _____

2. a. Take away a sound from the word **stroll** to make a word that means "a dwarf in a fairy tale."
   _____

   b. Take away two sounds from the word **stroll** to make a word that means "what a ball will do when it is pushed along the ground."

   _____

3. a. Take away a sound from the word **trace** to make a word that means "a running competition."
   _____

   b. Take away two sounds from the word **trace** to make a word that means "someone who is an expert at something."

   _____

4. a. Take away a sound from the word **swore** to make a word that means "was dressed in."
   _____

   b. Take away two sounds from the word **swore** to make a word that means "a mineral mined so that a valuable metal can be extracted."

   _____

Your Turn!

Directions: Select a word. Take away a sound—then two—to make new words.

Key Word	One Sound Taken Away	Two Sounds Taken Away
_____	_____	_____

UNIT 6

ADDITIONAL ACTIVITIES

CHANGE A SOUND

See how many words you can make by changing a sound—not a letter—in the word **wall.**

_____   _____

_____   _____

_____   _____

Next, see how many words you can make by changing a sound—not a letter—in the word **slip.**

_____   _____

_____   _____

_____   _____

Finally, see how many words you can make by changing a sound—not a letter—in the word **grass.**

_____   _____

_____   _____

_____   _____

ADDITIONAL ACTIVITIES

CHANGE A SOUND, THEN TWO

Activity 1

1. a. Change a sound in the word **grass** to make a word that means "a container that milk is poured into."

   _____

   b. Change two sounds in the word **grass** to make a word that means "happy."

   _____

2. a. Change a sound in the word **crow** to make a word that means "to get bigger."

   _____

   b. Change two sounds in the word **crow** to make a word that means "to shine or be incandescent."

   _____

3. a. Change a sound in the word **stamp** to make a word that means "the part of a tree left after its trunk is cut."

   _____

   b. Change two sounds in the word **stamp** to make a word that means "a drooping posture."

   _____

4. a. Change a sound in the word **click** to make a word that means "the sound a hen makes."

   _____

   b. Change two sounds in the word **click** to make a word that means "to adhere to."

   _____

Your Turn!

Directions: Select a word. Change a sound—then two—to make new words.

Key Word	One Sound Changed	Two Sounds Changed

CHANGE A SOUND, THEN TWO

Activity 2

1. a. Change a sound in the word *clam* to make a word that means "applaud."
    _____

    b. Change two sounds in the word *clam* to make a word that means "sad."
    _____

2. a. Change a sound in the word *spring* to make a word that means "a small cord used to tie packages."
    _____

    b. Change two sounds in the word *spring* to make a word that means "to begin to grow."
    _____

3. a. Change a sound in the word *chimp* to make a word that means "the person who is the winner."
    _____

    b. Change two sounds in the word *chimp* to make a word that means "an object that produces light."
    _____

4. a. Change a sound in the word *steam* to make a word that means "a secret plan of action."
    _____

    b. Change two sounds in the word *steam* to make a word that means "to move your foot forward."
    _____

Your Turn!

Directions: Select a word. Change a sound—then two—to make new words.

Key Word	One Sound Changed	Two Sounds Changed
_____	_____	_____

ADDITIONAL ACTIVITIES

ADD A SOUND

See how many words you can make by adding a sound—not a letter—to the word **bee.**

_____   _____

_____   _____

_____   _____

Next, see how many words you can make by adding a sound—not a letter—to the word **or.**

_____   _____

_____   _____

_____   _____

Finally, see how many words you can make by adding a sound—not a letter—to the word **in.**

_____   _____

_____   _____

_____   _____

UNIT 6	ADDITIONAL ACTIVITIES

ADD A SOUND, THEN TWO

Activity 1

1. a. Add a sound to the word **end** to make a word that means "to give something for temporary use and expect it to be returned."

    _____

    b. Add two sounds to the word **end** to make a word that means "to mix together."

    _____

2. a. Add a sound to the word **ink** to make a word that means "a segment of a chain."

    _____

    b. Add two sounds to the word **ink** to make a word that means "to quickly close and open one's eyes."

    _____

3. a. Add a sound to the word **and** to make a word that means "the solid part of the earth's surface."

    _____

    b. Add two sounds to the word **and** to make a word that means "not having much flavor."

    _____

4. a. Add a sound to the word **ever** to make a word that means "a bar used for prying."

    _____

    b. Add two sounds to the word **ever** to make a word that means "mentally quick and resourceful."

    _____

Your Turn!

Directions: Select a word. Add a sound—then two—to make new words.

Key Word	One Sound Added	Two Sounds Added
_____	_____	_____

> **UNIT 6**

> ### ADDITIONAL ACTIVITIES

> ## ADD A SOUND, THEN TWO

Activity 2

1. a. Add a sound to the word **ace** to make a word that means "a cord or string used to tie a shoe."
   _____

   b. Add two sounds to the word **ace** to make a word that means "to put something in a particular location."
   _____

2. a. Add a sound to the word **in** to make a word that means "one of the ten things to aim at in a bowling game."
   _____

   b. Add two sounds to the word **in** to make a word that means "to twirl about rapidly."
   _____

3. a. Add a sound to the word **ate** to make a word that means "after the proper time."
   _____

   b. Add two sounds to the word **ate** to make a word that means "something to put food on."
   _____

4. a. Add a sound to the word **end** to make a word that means "to watch over, to care for."
   _____

   b. Add two sounds to the word **end** to make a word that means "current style or preference."
   _____

Your Turn!

Directions: Select a word. Add a sound—then two—to make new words.

Key Word	One Sound Added	Two Sounds Added
_____	_____	_____

ADDITIONAL ACTIVITIES

TAKE AWAY, CHANGE, AND ADD A SOUND

Directions

Make new words by doing the following to each word listed:

	Take Away a Sound	Change a Sound	Add a Sound
1. leak			
2. play			
3. feast			
4. rail			
5. tray			
6. trip			
7. rod			
8. tear			
9. sill			
10. band			
11. stick			
12. maid			
13. miles			
14. grow			
15. creek			

Peter Pan

Directions

Change the name *Peter Pan* to fit each description that follows by adding one or more sounds to the word **Pan.** For example: Peter is a German tank. Peter Pan*zer.*

1. Peter resembles a bear. Peter Pan_____ .

2. Peter runs fast and is breathing hard. Peter Pan_____ .

3. Peter washes gravel from a stream to find gold. Peter Pan_____ .

4. Peter becomes very frightened and runs away. Peter Pan_____ .

5. Peter is a large, black leopard. Peter Pan_____ .

The Princess and the Pea

Directions

Retitle the story *The Princess and the Pea* to fit each description by adding one sound to the word **pea.** Remember, focus on the sounds of the word **pea**, not the spelling. For example: The princess had a feeling of resentment. *The Princess and the Peeve.*

1. The princess was skinning an orange. *The Princess and the* _____ .

2. The princess climbed a mountain. *The Princess and the* _____ .

3. The princess ate a piece of fruit with a pit. *The Princess and the* _____ .

4. The princess heard a baby chick. *The Princess and the* _____ .

5. The princess ended a war. *The Princess and the* _____ .

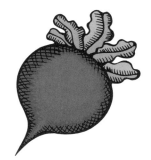

ADDITIONAL ACTIVITIES

WORDS WiTH THREE SOUNDS

Directions to Facilitator

Have students come up with as many words with three sounds as they can. Have them write their responses on the blank line that follows each word, or you may write their responses on a blackboard or transparency. Remind students that the number of letters in a word may not be the same as the number of sounds and that the spelling of the sounds may change.

Example 1

/b _ t/   *bit, bat, but, bet, bait, beet, bite, boat, bout, bought*

/t _ _ /   *tip, ten, taught, ton tap, tan, tin, tape, taupe, take, tail, tell, tile*

/_ _ p/   *cup, cap, lip, lap, map, mop, tip, tap, top, sip, soap, loop, rope, tape*

Words with Three Sounds

1. /p _ t/   _____

2. /s _ d/   _____

3. /r _ _ /   _____

4. /v _ _ /   _____

5. /_ _ k/   _____

6. /_ _ m/   _____

7. /l _ _ /   _____

8. /_ _ f/   _____

9. /w _ _ /   _____

10. /_ _ g/   _____

ADDITIONAL ACTIVITIES

WORDS WITH FOUR SOUNDS

Directions to Facilitator

Have students come up with as many words with four sounds as they can. Have them write their responses on the blank line that follows each word, or you may write their responses on a blackboard or transparency. Remind students that the number of letters in a word may not be the same as the number of sounds and that the spelling of the sounds may change.

Example 1

/b _ _ d/   *brad, bold, bald, band, breed, bread, braid, brood, board, barred*

/g _ _ _ /   *glum, gift, grade, group, grape, grain, glass, glaze, ghost, guessed*

/_ _ _ t/   *brat, trot, past, pest, best, boast, baste, treat, great, cost, brought*

/tr _ _ /   *trap, trip, trail, trial, trade, train, trace, truce, truth, trick, track*

Words with Four Sounds

1. /k _ _ n/ _____

2. /s _ _ n/ _____

3. /l _ _ _ / _____

4. /r _ _ _ / _____

5. /_ _ _ p/ _____

6. /_ _ _ k/ _____

7. /st _ _ / _____

8. /pr _ _ / _____

9. /sl _ _ / _____

10. /tr _ _ / _____

ADDITIONAL ACTIVITIES

KNOCK-KNOCK JOKES

Activity 1

Directions: Find the word or words that have one or more sound changes. Then, find the real word(s) in each of the following knock-knock jokes.

1. Knock, knock. *Who's there?*
    Jimmy. *Jimmy who?*
    Jimmy a little kiss.

    Word with sound change:

    _____

    Word before sound change:

    _____

2. Knock, knock. *Who's there?*
    Izzy. *Izzy who?*
    Izzy come, Izzy go.

    Word with sound change:

    _____

    Word before sound change:

    _____

3. Knock, knock. *Who's there?*
    Jaws. *Jaws who?*
    Jaws truly.

    Word with sound change:

    _____

    Word before sound change:

    _____

4. Knock, knock. *Who's there?*
    Kent. *Kent who?*
    Kent you tell who it is?

    Word with sound change:

    _____

    Word before sound change:

    _____

Your Turn!

Directions: Make up a knock-knock joke and tell it to a friend!

Knock, knock. *Who's there?*

_____ .

_____ who?

_____ .

Word(s) with sound change(s):

_____

Word(s) before sound change(s):

_____

KNOCK-KNOCK JOKES

Activity 2

Directions: Find the word or words that have one or more sound changes. Then, find the real word(s) in each of the following knock-knock jokes.

1. Knock, knock. *Who's there?*
    Leif. *Leif who?*
    Leif me alone.

    Word with sound change:

    _____

    Word before sound change:

    _____

2. Knock, knock. *Who's there?*
    Nettie. *Nettie who?*
    Nettie as a fruitcake.

    Word with sound change:

    _____

    Word before sound change:

    _____

3. Knock, knock. *Who's there?*
    Shirley. *Shirley who?*
    Shirley, you must know me by now.

    Word with sound change:

    _____

    Word before sound change:

    _____

4. Knock, knock. *Who's there?*
    Vaughn. *Vaughn who?*
    Vaughn day my prince will come.

    Word with sound change:

    _____

    Word before sound change:

    _____

Your Turn!

Directions: Make up a knock-knock joke and tell it to a friend!

Knock, knock. *Who's there?*

_____ .

_____ who?

_____ .

Word(s) with sound change(s):

_____

Word(s) before sound change(s):

_____

ADDITIONAL ACTIVITIES

KNOCK-KNOCK JOKES

Activity 3

Directions: Find the word or words that have one or more sound changes. Then, find the real word(s) in each of the following knock-knock jokes.

1. Knock, knock. *Who's there?*
    Voodoo. *Voodoo who?*
    Voodoo you think you are?

    Word with sound change:

    _____

    Words before sound change:

    _____

2. Knock, knock. *Who's there?*
    Whittle. *Whittle who?*
    Whittle Orphan Annie.

    Word with sound change:

    _____

    Word before sound change:

    _____

3. Knock, knock. *Who's there?*
    Yelp. *Yelp who?*
    Yelp me! My nose is stuck in the door.

    Word with sound change:

    _____

    Word before sound change:

    _____

4. Knock, knock. *Who's there?*
    Yachts. *Yachts who?*
    Yachts up, Doc?

    Word with sound change:

    _____

    Word before sound change:

    _____

Your Turn!

Directions: Make up a knock-knock joke and tell it to a friend!

Knock, knock. *Who's there?*

_____ .

_____ who?

_____ .

Word(s) with sound change(s):

_____

Word(s) before sound change(s):

_____

UNIT 6 — ADDITIONAL ACTIVITIES

KNOCK-KNOCK JOKES

Activity 4

Directions: Find the word or words that have one or more sound changes. Then, find the real word(s) in each of the following knock-knock jokes.

1. Knock, knock. *Who's there?*
    Safe. *Safe who?*
    Safe these cookies for later. I'm full.

    Word with sound change:

    _____

    Word before sound change:

    _____

2. Knock, knock. *Who's there?*
    Sid. *Sid who?*
    Sid down. It's time to eat.

    Word with sound change:

    _____

    Word before sound change:

    _____

3. Knock, knock. *Who's there?*
    Free. *Free who?*
    Free o'clock. School's out.

    Word with sound change:

    _____

    Word before sound change:

    _____

4. Knock, knock. *Who's there?*
    Zeke. *Zeke who?*
    Zeke and ye shall find.

    Word with sound change:

    _____

    Word before sound change:

    _____

Your Turn!

Directions: Make up a knock-knock joke and tell it to a friend!

Knock, knock. *Who's there?*

_____ .

_____ who?

_____ .

Word(s) with sound change(s):

_____

Word(s) before sound change(s):

_____

ADDITIONAL ACTIVITIES

KNOCK-KNOCK JOKES

Activity 5

Directions: Find the word or words that have one or more sound changes. Then, find the real word(s) in each of the following knock-knock jokes.

1. Knock, knock. *Who's there?*
   Pet. *Pet who?*
   Pet another penny in my purse.

   Word with sound change:

   _____

   Word before sound change:

   _____

2. Knock, knock. *Who's there?*
   Salon. *Salon who?*
   Salon. It's been good to know you.

   Word with sound change:

   _____

   Word before sound change:

   _____

3. Knock, knock. *Who's there?*
   Fanny. *Fanny who?*
   Fannybody home?

   Word with sound change:

   _____

   Word before sound change:

   _____

4. Knock, knock. *Who's there?*
   Freddie. *Freddie who?*
   Freddie or not, here I come.

   Word with sound change:

   _____

   Word before sound change:

   _____

Your Turn!

Directions: Make up a knock-knock joke and tell it to a friend!

Knock, knock. *Who's there?*

_____ .

_____ who?

_____ .

Word(s) with sound change(s):

_____

Word(s) before sound change(s):

_____

KNOCK-KNOCK JOKES

Activity 6

Directions: Find the word or words that have one or more sound changes. Then, find the real word(s) in each of the following knock-knock jokes.

1. Knock, knock. *Who's there?*
    Harry. *Harry who?*
    Harry up. We're late.

    Word with sound change:

    _____

    Word before sound change:

    _____

2. Knock, knock. *Who's there?*
    Myth. *Myth who?*
    Myth you, too.

    Word with sound change:

    _____

    Word before sound change:

    _____

3. Knock, knock. *Who's there?*
    Scissor. *Scissor who?*
    Scissor and Cleopatra.

    Word with sound change:

    _____

    Word before sound change:

    _____

4. Knock, knock. *Who's there?*
    Barton. *Barton who?*
    Barton up your overcoat.

    Word with sound change:

    _____

    Word before sound change:

    _____

Your Turn!

Directions: Make up a knock-knock joke and tell it to a friend!

Knock, knock. *Who's there?*

_____ .

_____ who?

_____ .

Word(s) with sound change(s):

_____

Word(s) before sound change(s):

_____

UNIT 6

ADDITIONAL ACTIVITIES

KNOCK-KNOCK JOKES

Activity 7

Directions: Find the word or words that have one or more sound changes. Then, find the real word(s) in each of the following knock-knock jokes.

1. Knock, knock. *Who's there?*
    Dwayne. *Dwayne who?*
    Dwayne the tub. I'm dwowning!

    Word with sound change:

    _____

    Word before sound change:

    _____

2. Knock, knock. *Who's there?*
    Luke. *Luke who?*
    Luke before you leap.

    Word with sound change:

    _____

    Word before sound change:

    _____

3. Knock, knock. *Who's there?*
    Don. *Don who?*
    Don eat all the turkey. I want some.

    Word with sound change:

    _____

    Word before sound change:

    _____

4. Knock, knock. *Who's there?*
    Ears. *Ears who?*
    Ears looking at you, kid.

    Word with sound change:

    _____

    Word before sound change:

    _____

Your Turn!

Directions: Make up a knock-knock joke and tell it to a friend!

Knock, knock. *Who's there?*

_____ .

_____ who?

_____ .

Word(s) with sound change(s):

_____

Word(s) before sound change(s):

_____

Activity 8

Directions: Find the word or words that have one or more sound changes. Then, find the real word(s) in each of the following knock-knock jokes.

1. Knock, knock. *Who's there?*
    Tars. *Tars who?*
    Tars and tripes forever.

    Words with sound changes:
    _____

    Words before sound changes:
    _____

2. Knock, knock. *Who's there?*
    Sarah. *Sarah who?*
    Sarah good show on TV tonight?

    Word with sound changes:
    _____

    Words before sound changes:
    _____

3. Knock, knock. *Who's there?*
    Noman. *Noman who?*
    Noman is an island.

    Word with sound change:
    _____

    Words before sound change:
    _____

4. Knock, knock. *Who's there?*
    Gladys. *Gladys who?*
    Gladys not raining!

    Word with sound change:
    _____

    Words before sound change:
    _____

Your Turn!

Directions: Make up a knock-knock joke and tell it to a friend!

Knock, knock. *Who's there?*

_____ .

_____ who?

_____ .

Word(s) with sound change(s):

_____

Word(s) before sound change(s):

_____

ANSWER KEY

ANSWER KEY

UNIT 1: TAKE AWAY A CONSONANT SOUND
Warm-Up Activities

Activity 1
1. ice
2. oil
3. end
4. eel
5. old
6. ear
7. ill
8. oat

Activity 2
1. flee
2. lie
3. bay
4. bass
5. tie
6. fee
7. flow
8. go

Activity 3
1. lap
2. trip
3. wine
4. lake
5. raise
6. late
7. cold
8. poke

Activity 4
1. all
2. eat
3. ail
4. lick
5. oak
6. inch
7. ring
8. rain

Activity 1 Review
1. peel
2. moat
3. /l/
4. /n/
5. pill
6. /t/ /ɛ/ /n/ /d/
7. mold
8. /m/

Activity 2 Review
1. /b/ /eɪ/ /s/ /t/
2. /n/
3. /p/
4. float
5. /t/
6. /g/ /oʊ/ /t/
7. bake
8. /f/

Activity 3 Review
1. praise
2. /k/
3. /f/ /l/ /eɪ/ /k/
4. /f/
5. scold
6. /s/
7. twine
8. /s/ /t/ /r/ /ɪ/ /p/

Activity 4 Review
1. click
2. bring
3. /l/
4. /r/
5. /f/
6. /s/ /ɪ/ /n/ /tʃ/
7. /t/
8. folk

UNIT 1: TAKE AWAY A CONSONANT SOUND
Phonological Humor Activities

Activity 1
1. a. Ape
    b. A
    c. *gorilla* and *learns in school*
    d. A gorilla is a type of ape, and we learn the ABCs (alphabet) in school.

2. a. Hare
    b. Air
    c. *rabbit, do when he grew up,* and *Force*
    d. A rabbit is a type of hare, and *Hare Force* sounds like *Air Force,* which many young adults join for employment.

3. a. Burp
    b. Earp
    c. *western hero* and *noise at dinner*
    d. Wyatt Earp was a hero in the American West during the last century, and *Earp* sounds like *burp,* which is a loud sound people sometimes make while or after they eat.

Activity 2
1. a. mice
    b. ice
    c. *sport, mice, athletes,* and *hockey*
    d. Ice (which sounds like *mice*) is the surface that hockey is played on, hockey is a sport, and athletes participate in sports.

2. a. hair
    b. air
    c. *wigs* and *mail*
    d. A letter can be sent by air mail, and wigs are made of hair.

3. a. toad-dancing
    b. toe-dancing
    c. *tadpole* and *little, pink, satin slippers*
    d. A tadpole is a baby toad (which sounds like toe), and people take lessons for toe dancing, often while wearing little, pink, satin slippers.

UNIT 1: TAKE AWAY A CONSONANT SOUND
Phonological Humor Activities (continued)

Activity 3

1. a. hoptometrist
   b. optometrist
   c. *frog* and *glasses*
   d. Frogs hop, optometrists sell glasses, and *hoptometrist* sound like *optometrist.*

2. a. hencyclopedia
   b. encyclopedia
   c. *book* and *chickens*
   d. A hen is a female chicken, an encyclopedia is a reference book, and *hencyclopedia* sounds like *encyclopedia.*

3. a. José Canusi
   b. Oh, say can you see
   c. name and "The Star-Spangled Banner"
   d. José Canusi is a name, and the first line of "The Star-Spangled Banner" begins with "Oh, say can you see," which sounds like *José Canusi.*

Activity 4

1. a. hambulance
   b. ambulance
   c. *pig* and *go to the hospital*
   d. An ambulance is a vehicle that goes to and from hospitals, ham is a meat that comes from pigs, and *hambulance* sounds like *ambulance.*

2. a. hentertainment
   b. entertainment
   c. *chicken show*
   d. A hen is a female chicken, you go to a show to be entertained, and *hentertainment* sounds like *entertainment.*

3. a. kung food
   b. kung fu
   c. *sweet-and-sour* and *kicks*
   d. Chinese foods often are cooked in a sweet-and-sour sauce; *kung fu* refers to the Chinese martial arts, in which people kick; and *food* sounds like *fu.*

Activity 5

1. a. broommates
   b. roommates
   c. *witches* and *live together*
   d. Witches ride on brooms, and roommates (which sounds like *broommates*) share living quarters.

2. a. Stinkerbell
   b. Tinkerbell
   c. *fairy* and *smelled bad*
   d. *Stinkerbell* sounds like *Tinkerbell,* who is a fairy in Peter Pan; and *stink* means "to smell bad."

3. a. grab
   b. gab
   c. *shoplifter*
   d. Shoplifters steal (grab) things, and *gift of grab* sounds like *gift of gab* (the ability to talk a lot).

Activity 6

1. a. foundling
   b. founding
   c. *George Washington* and *orphan*
   d. Washington has been called "the founding father of his country" (USA), and *foundling* is another word for *orphan.*

2. a. clause
   b. cause
   c. *contract, read the fine print,* and *suspicion*
   d. When a section of writing (clause) in a contract is written in fine (very small) print, the writer may not want the reader to be aware of what it says. This should be a cause for suspicion, which sounds like *clause for suspicion.*

3. a. Scream
   b. Cream
   c. *ghouls* and *breakfast*
   d. Ghouls are scary and make you scream (which sounds like *cream*), and Cream of Wheat is a breakfast cereal.

UNIT 1: TAKE AWAY A CONSONANT SOUND
Phonological Humor Activities (continued)

Activity 7

1. a. sturgeon
   b. surgeon
   c. *operations* and *fish hospital*
   d. Surgeons operate at hospitals, and *sturgeon* (a type of fish) sounds like *surgeon.*

2. a. bestsmeller
   b. bestseller
   c. *book, didn't like,* and *critic*
   d. Critics rave about books they like and they become bestsellers. Books they do not like can be called "bestsmellers" because *smell* is another way of saying that something is bad.

3. a. corpse
   b. course
   c. *zombies* and *dead*
   d. A zombie is a corpse (a dead body), and *corpse* sounds like *course.*

Activity 8

1. a. glove
   b. love
   c. *baseball player, sing,* and *mitt*
   d. A baseball player's mitt is also called a *glove,* and people sing love songs (which sounds like *glove songs*).

2. a. Proof
   b. Roof
   c. *editor* and *Fiddler*
   d. Editors proofread documents and fiddle with words to make corrections before publication, and *Fiddler on the Proof* sounds like *Fiddler on the Roof,* which is the title of a movie and play.

3. a. spray
   b. pray
   c. *skunk* and *cornered*
   d. Skunks spray a terrible smelling scent when they are cornered (in a frightening situation), and "Let us spray" sounds like the expression "Let us pray."

Activity 9

1. a. glow
   b. go
   c. *teacher, excuse,* and *firefly*
   d. Teachers excuse children who need to leave the classroom to go to the bathroom, and fireflies glow (which sounds like *go*).

2. a. flounder
   b. founder
   c. *George Washington* and *fish*
   d. Washington has been called the founder of his country (USA), and a flounder (which sounds like *founder*) is a fish.

3. a. scream
   b. cream
   c. *witch, sugar,* and *coffee*
   d. Witches make people scream (which sounds like *cream*); and cream, like sugar, is often put into coffee.

Activity 10

1. a. vroomatism
   b. rheumatism
   c. *disease* and *racing cars*
   d. Rheumatism (which sounds like *vroomatism*) is a disease, and racing cars make a "vroom" sound as they speed by.

2. a. friar
   b. fire
   c. *egg, monastery,* and *frying pan*
   d. A friar (which sounds like *fire*) often lives in a monastery, an egg can be cooked in a frying pan, and "Out of the frying pan, into the fire" is a common expression.

3. a. baldpoint
   b. ballpoint
   c. *eagle, write,* and *pen*
   d. The bald eagle is a type of eagle, and many pens are ballpoint.

UNIT 1: TAKE AWAY A CONSONANT SOUND
Phonological Humor Activities (continued)

Activity 11

1. a. drill
    b. dill
    c. *pickle* and *dentist*
    d. Dill is a kind of pickle, and dentists drill, which sounds like *dill.*

2. a. Twinnie
    b. Winnie
    c. *Winnie the Pooh* and *identical brother*
    d. An identical brother is likely to be a twin, and *Twinnie the Pooh* sounds like *Winnie the Pooh,* a familiar childhood character.

3. a. Pizza
    b. Pisa
    c. *stacked thousands of pizzas*
    d. If someone stacked thousands of pizzas on top of each other, the pile would probably lean to one side; and *Leaning Tower of Pizza* sounds like *Leaning Tower of Pisa,* which is a famous structure in Italy.

Activity 12

1. a. plop
    b. pop
    c. *raindrop* and *say to the other raindrop*
    d. *Plop* is the sound made by raindrops when they fall, and the phrase given sounds like the childish taunt "My pop is bigger than your pop."

2. a. skid
    b. kid
    c. *adults* and *ice*
    d. Ice causes skids, and *skid stuff* sounds like the common phrase *kid stuff.*

3. a. fright
    b. fight
    c. *ghost* and *join the navy*
    d. Ghosts give people a fright, one would join the navy to fight for one's country, and *fright* sounds like *fight.*

Activity 13

1. a. hamburglar
    b. hamburger
    c. *thief* and *steals meat*
    d. *Burglar* is another word for *thief,* a person who steals things; and hamburger, which sounds like *hamburglar,* is a kind of meat.

2. a. slide
    b. side
    c. *cross the microscope*
    d. Slides are examined under a microscope, and *to get to the other side* (which sounds like *to get to the other slide*) is a well-known response to the joke "Why did the chicken cross the road?"

3. a. frighter
    b. fighter
    c. *referee* and *ghost boxing match*
    d. A ghost is supposed to frighten people, *frighter* sounds like *fighter,* and often referees say "May the best fighter win" at the beginning of boxing matches.

UNIT 2: CHANGE A CONSONANT SOUND
Warm-Up Activities

Activity 1	**Activity 2**	**Activity 3**	**Activity 4**
1. sick	1. trick	1. snake	1. breed
2. light	2. grin	2. stale	2. mask
3. honey	3. drove	3. smoke	3. grass
4. jet	4. skin	4. blush	4. comb
5. round	5. page	5. skunk	5. fix
6. sink	6. clock	6. snack	6. rust
7. mouse	7. creep	7. clone	7. stain
8. sad	8. juice	8. spout	8. nape

Activity 1 Review	**Activity 2 Review**	**Activity 3 Review**	**Activity 4 Review**
1. night	1. no	1. smack	1. /r/
2. /l/ /ɛ/ /t/	2. /d/ /r/ /oʊ/ /n/	2. crone	2. /n/
3. /m/	3. /t/	3. /b/ /r/ /ʌ/ /ʃ/	3. /g/ /l/ /æ/ /s/
4. yes	4. paid	4. /k/	4. mix
5. /s/	5. /n/	5. /p/	5. /r/
6. /θ/	6. clot	6. yes	6. /h/
7. /p/ /æ/ /d/	7. /s/	7. /s/ /t/ /ʌ/ /ŋ/ /k/	7. tape
8. money	8. /d/	8. scale	8. no

UNIT 2: CHANGE A CONSONANT SOUND
Phonological Humor Activities

Activity 1

1. a. Moos
    b. News
    c. *newspaper* and *cows*
    d. *The Daily Moos* sounds like *The Daily News,* and a cow moos.

2. a. anther
    b. answer
    c. *called* and *panther*
    d. A call usually requires an answer; and *anther,* which rhymes with *panther,* sounds like *answer.*

3. a. copsicle
    b. popsicle
    c. *frozen* and *police officer*
    d. *Cop* is another word for police officer, and *copsicle* sounds like *popsicle,* a frozen treat on a stick.

Activity 2

1. a. oinkment
    b. ointment
    c. *cure* and *sick hog*
    d. Ointments are used to treat sickness, a hog oinks, and *oinkment* sounds like *ointment.*

2. a. womb
    b. room
    c. *newborn infant*
    d. The infant came from the womb (uterus), *quarters* refers to living space (room), and *womb service* sounds like *room service.*

3. a. shellfish
    b. selfish
    c. *clam* and *doesn't share*
    d. A clam is a shellfish, which sounds like *selfish,* a quality of someone who doesn't share.

UNIT 2: CHANGE A CONSONANT SOUND
Phonological Humor Activities (Continued)

Activity 3

1. a. barking
    b. parking
    c. *dogs* and *shopping*
    d. Dogs bark; and *barking lot* sounds like *parking lot,* which is found at a shopping mall.

2. a. Ghost
    b. Coast
    c. *do when he grew up* and *join*
    d. A young adult might join the Coast Guard as a career choice, and *ghost* sounds like *coast.*

3. a. harp
    b. heart
    c. *angel, very ill,* and *attack*
    d. Angels often are shown playing harps, and *harp attack* sounds like *heart attack,* which makes you very ill.

Activity 4

1. a. pace
    b. face
    c. *racehorse*
    d. Racehorses run at a particular pace, and "your pace is familiar" sounds like "your face is familiar."

2. a. bite
    b. sight
    c. *Dracula*
    d. Dracula is known for biting, and *love at first bite* sounds like the expression *love at first sight.*

3. a. Boulders
    b. Shoulders
    c. *shampoo* and *mountains*
    d. Head and Shoulders is the name of a shampoo; *shoulders* sounds like *boulders,* which is another word for large rocks; and boulders can be found on mountains.

Activity 5

1. a. bat
    b. bad
    c. *Batman* and *brush his teeth*
    d. Batman is dressed like a bat, which sounds like *bad,* and one reason you brush your teeth is to prevent bad breath.

2. a. fleas
    b. fleece
    c. *lamb*
    d. Lambs have fleece, which sound like *fleas.*

3. a. cello
    b. Jell-O
    c. *comes in different flavors and colors* and *makes music*
    d. A cello is a musical instrument, and *cello* sound like *Jell-O,* which comes in different flavors and colors.

Activity 6

1. a. hiss
    b. kiss
    c. *boy snake* and *girl snake*
    d. Boys and girls kiss, and *kiss* sounds like *hiss,* which is what snakes do.

2. a. tweetment
    b. treatment
    c. *sick bird* and *first-aid*
    d. A bird says *tweet,* which sounds like *treat,* and first-aid treatment is given when someone is sick or has a medical problem.

3. a. quackers
    b. crackers
    c. *cross cows and ducks* and *milk*
    d. Cows give milk, ducks quack, and *milk and quackers* sounds like *milk and crackers.*

UNiT 2: CHANGE A CONSONANT SOUND
Phonological Humor Activities (Continued)

Activity 7
1. a. sweep
   b. sleep
   c. *mother broom* and *infant broom*
   d. Brooms sweep, and "go to sweep" sounds like "go to sleep," which is something a mother says to a baby.

2. a. hearth
   b. heart
   c. *fireplace, hospital,* and *attack*
   d. A fireplace has a hearth around it, and *hearth attack* sounds like *heart attack,* for which you are likely to be in a hospital.

3. a. mouse
   b. house
   c. *exterminator*
   d. Exterminators are called to get rid of mice, and *mouse calls* sounds like *house calls,* which are sometimes made by doctors.

Activity 9
1. a. Voltswagon
   b. Volkswagen
   c. *car* and *electrician*
   d. *Voltswagon* sounds like *Volkswagen,* a type of car; and electricians work with voltage.

2. a. westing
   b. resting
   c. *sleeping* and *Westinghouse*
   d. A company called Westinghouse made refrigerators, and *westing* sounds like *resting.*

3. a. Tide
   b. side
   c. *Eskimos* and *wash in Tide*
   d. Eskimos live in Alaska, which is very cold, so it would be too cold to wash clothes outside; *outside* sound like *out Tide* (the opposite of in Tide); and Tide is a laundry detergent.

Activity 8
1. a. flies
   b. fries
   c. *spiders, hamburgers,* and *French*
   d. Spiders eat flies, which sounds like *fries,* and hamburgers often are served with French fries.

2. a. wheel
   b. real
   c. *sells mobile homes* and *estate broker*
   d. Mobile homes are on wheels, someone who sells homes is called a real estate broker, and *wheel* sounds like *real.*

3. a. cloud
   b. crowd
   c. *raindrop* and *other raindrop*
   d. Raindrops fall from a cloud, and *cloud* sound like *crowd,* as in "Two's company, three's a crowd."

Activity 10
1. a. quack
   b. crack
   c. *duck* and *sharpshooting*
   d. Ducks quack, which sounds like *crack,* and a sharpshooter is a crack shot (superior marksman).

2. a. Sulk
   b. Hulk
   c. *big, green, and doesn't speak all day* and *Incredible*
   d. The Incredible Hulk is big and green; *sulk* sounds like *Hulk;* and sulk means "to mope around not speaking to anyone."

3. a. firequacker
   b. firecracker
   c. *duck* and *Fourth of July*
   d. Ducks say quack, which sounds like *crack;* and on the Fourth of July, people use firecrackers.

UNiT 3: CHANGE A VOWEL SOUND
Warm-Up Activities

Activity 1
1. road
2. back
3. bat
4. bug
5. lamp
6. truck
7. rug
8. bowl

Activity 2
1. well
2. trap
3. dam
4. fail
5. blank
6. fire
7. cat
8. gnat

Activity 3
1. baste
2. pool
3. chore
4. moat
5. chess
6. moth
7. moan
8. green

Activity 4
1. troop
2. vague
3. wand
4. tack
5. spice
6. pest
7. jolly
8. tame

Activity 1 Review
1. no
2. /b/ /ɔ/ /t/
3. /oʊ/
4. bag
5. /oʊ/
6. limp
7. /b/
8. /æ/

Activity 2 Review
1. foil
2. trip
3. /w/ /ɪ/ /l/
4. yes
5. knit
6. /ɑɪ/
7. /ɪ/
8. /k/

Activity 3 Review
1. cheer
2. /oʊ/
3. /p/ /ɪ/ /l/
4. chose
5. mouth
6. no
7. /g/
8. /m/ /æ/ /n/

Activity 4 Review
1. /s/ /p/ /eɪ/ /s/
2. yes
3. vogue
4. /m/
5. /ɑ/
6. trap
7. /æ/
8. /w/

UNiT 3: CHANGE A VOWEL SOUND
Phonological Humor Activities

Activity 1
1. a. Feather
   b. Father
   c. *baby birds* and *parents*
   d. Baby birds have fathers and feathers, and *feather* sounds like *father.*

2. a. pence
   b. pants
   c. *shillings* and *pence*
   d. They are names for money in England, and *pence* sounds like *pants,* which should be worn when walking down the street.

3. a. illigator
   b. alligator
   c. *sick* and *relative of a crocodile*
   d. An alligator is a relative of a crocodile, and *ill* is another word for *sick.*

Activity 2
1. a. haunting
   b. hunting
   c. *ghosts* and *stop scaring people*
   d. Ghosts are thought to haunt people; and *haunting license* sounds like *hunting license,* which is needed to hunt.

2. a. mummies
   b. mommies
   c. *Egyptian children*
   d. Egyptians preserved the dead by making them into mummies, and *mummies* sounds like *mommies.*

3. a. buzzy
   b. busy
   c. *phoning, bee,* and *signal*
   d. Bees buzz, and *buzzy signal* sounds like *busy signal,* which is an annoying sound that can be heard on the phone.

UNIT 3: CHANGE A VOWEL SOUND
Phonological Humor Activities (Continued)

Activity 3
1. a. cluck
   b. clock
   c. *clock, chicken,* and *alarm*
   d. Clocks have alarms, and chickens cluck, which sounds like *clock.*

2. a. Elka-Seltzer
   b. Alka-Seltzer
   c. *elk with indigestion*
   d. *Elka-Seltzer* sounds like *Alka-Seltzer,* which is a medication taken for indigestion.

3. a. chap
   b. chip
   c. *acrobat*
   d. Acrobats often balance people on their shoulders, *chap* is a British word for *man* or *boy,* and "had a chap on his shoulder" sounds like the expression "had a chip on his shoulder."

Activity 4
1. a. unhoppy
   b. unhappy
   c. *doesn't a frog jump* and *sad*
   d. *Hop* is another word for *jump;* frogs usually hop; and *sad* means "unhappy," which sounds like *unhoppy.*

2. a. poodle
   b. puddle
   c. *raining cats and dogs* and *stepped in*
   d. The expression "raining cats and dogs" means "raining heavily"; and rain causes puddles, which sounds like *poodles,* a breed of dog.

3. a. jungle
   b. jingle
   c. *Tarzan, sing,* and *Christmastime*
   d. Tarzan is a fictional character who lives in the jungle, and *jungle* sounds like *jingle,* as in the Christmas song "Jingle Bells."

UNIT 4: ADD A CONSONANT SOUND
Warm-Up Activities

Activity 1	Activity 2	Activity 3	Activity 4
1. tooth	1. sore	1. slush	1. grip
2. hive	2. howl	2. frail	2. flaw
3. guide	3. weed	3. brag	3. tend
4. save	4. mane	4. prank	4. stale
5. sign	5. peel	5. gasp	5. trust
6. cape	6. bend	6. tint	6. mold
7. pup	7. dill	7. charm	7. steam
8. boat	8. rink	8. brave	8. grope

Activity 1 Review	Activity 2 Review	Activity 3 Review	Activity 4 Review
1. /p/	1. /k/	1. gas	1. /d/
2. sigh	2. /l/	2. /tʃ/	2. /p/
3. yes	3. owl	3. yes	3. rust
4. /t/	4. may	4. /r/	4. no
5. say	5. /ɪ/ /l/	5. lush	5. seem
6. /t/	6. /s/	6. /b/ /oʊ/ /l/	6. /l/
7. no	7. end	7. bag	7. no
8. /v/	8. no	8. /t/	8. sale

UNIT 4: ADD A CONSONANT SOUND
Phonological Humor Activities

Activity 1

1. a. hopsichord
   b. harpsichord
   c. *frog* and *musical instrument*
   d. Frogs hop, and *hopsichord* sounds like *harpsichord,* which is a musical instrument.

2. a. sink
   b. stink
   c. *swimming team* and *swam very badly*
   d. When someone does something very badly, you could say that he or she "stinks." Swimming very badly could cause you to sink, which sounds like *stink.*

3. a. code
   b. cold
   c. *secret agent* and *take two aspirins and go to bed*
   d. Secret agents use codes, which sounds like *colds,* and doctors tell patients to take two aspirins and go to bed when they have a cold.

Activity 3

1. a. ape
   b. tape
   c. *gather information* and *recorder*
   d. *Ape* sounds like *tape,* and tape recorders are used to store information.

2. a. sick-shooter
   b. six-shooter
   c. *cowboys* and *doctor's hypodermic needle*
   d. In movies and television shows, a cowboy carried a gun called a six-shooter, which sounds like *sick-shooter,* and a doctor's hypodermic needle is used for giving shots of medicine to sick people.

3. a. Rover
   b. Grover
   c. *president* and *dogcatcher*
   d. Grover Cleveland was one of the presidents of the United States, and *Grover* sounds like *Rover,* which is a common name for a dog.

Activity 2

1. a. cattleloupe
   b. cantaloupe
   c. *cow* and *fruit*
   d. Cows as a group are called *cattle,* and *cattleoupe* sounds like *cantaloupe,* which is a kind of fruit.

2. a. Eds
   b. heads
   c. *Ed* and *Ed also*
   d. If Ellen's husband and son are both named Ed, she would have two Eds in her family. "Two Eds are better than one" sounds like the expression "Two heads are better than one."

3. a. team
   b. steam
   c. *game* and *showers*
   d. Players need to shower after a game, hot showers produce steam, and *team* sounds like *steam.*

Activity 4

1. a. booberry
   b. blueberry
   c. *ghost's* and *dessert*
   d. Ghosts say "boo," which sounds like *blue,* and blueberry pie is a favorite dessert for many people.

2. a. dive-in
   b. drive-in
   c. *movie house* and *swimming pool*
   d. Some movies are shown in drive-in theaters, and *drive-in* sounds like *dive-in,* which is what one can do at a swimming pool.

3. a. top, tep
   b. stop, step
   c. *top, car,* and *brake*
   d. To stop a car, you step on the brake, and since *stop* without an s becomes *top,* it is likely that *tep* has the same sound missing.

UNIT 5: CHALLENGE ACTIVITIES

Activity 1

1. a. discus
    b. disk
    c. *Olympic athletes, injury,* and *slipped discus*
    d. One event at the Olympics is discus throwing, and some people injure their backs when a spinal disk slips out of place.

2. a. mutton
    b. nothing (nothin')
    c. *sheep* and *mutton in common*
    d. Mutton is the flesh of a mature sheep, and *mutton in common* sounds like the expression "nothing in common."

3. a. squid
    b. kid
    c. *lives in the ocean, tentacles,* and *quick on the draw*
    d. A squid lives in the ocean and has tentacles, and *Billy the Squid* sounds like *Billy the Kid,* who was a notorious western outlaw known for his ability to draw his gun very quickly.

Activity 2

1. a. parsley
    b. Presley
    c. *green, sings,* and *Elvis*
    d. *Elvis Parsley* sounds like *Elvis Presley,* a famous singer; and parsley is a green herb.

2. a. neak, tame
    b. sneak, same
    c. *catch, unique,* and *tame*
    d. *You neak up on it* sounds like *you sneak up on it,* which is often the way to catch an animal; *unique* sounds like *you neak;* and *tame* sounds like *same.*

3. a. weeping
    b. sleeping
    c. *sad sister* and *Sleeping Beauty*
    d. Sadness may cause weeping, and Sleeping Beauty's sister also would have Beauty as her last name.

Activity 3

1. a. feelers
    b. feelings
    c. *insult* and *alien*
    d. Aliens are sometimes pictured with feelers, and often one's feelings are hurt following an insult.

2. a. coinivorous
    b. carnivorous
    c. *doesn't return your money* and *vending machine*
    d. A broken machine often will take (eat) your coins and not give you a drink in return, and a carnivorous animal (one that eats meat) can be dangerous, so you have to beware.

3. a. foods and morsels
    b. fools and mortals
    c. *restaurant*
    d. Restaurants serve morsels of food, and "What foods these morsels be" sounds like "What fools these mortals be," which is a famous line written by Shakespeare.

Activity 4

1. a. sheepovers
    b. sleepovers
    c. *birthday parties* and *lamb*
    d. Sometimes birthday parties involve sleepovers, and a lamb is a young sheep.

2. a. platter
    b. matter
    c. *dieting*
    d. When you diet, you think about food a lot; food is often served on a platter; and "mind over platter" sounds like "mind over matter," a common expression.

3. a. spyfocals
    b. bifocals
    c. *James Bond* and *glasses*
    d. Bond is a well-known fictional spy, bifocals are a type of glasses, and *spyfocals* sounds like *bifocals.*

UNIT 5: CHALLENGE ACTIVITIES

Activity 5

1. a. horsepital
    b. hospital
    c. *sick pony*
    d. A pony is a small horse, and *horsepital* sounds like *hospital,* which is where sick people often need to go.

2. a. coffin
    b. coughing
    c. *Dracula* and *do when he has a cold*
    d. Dracula sleeps in a coffin; when people have a cold, they cough a lot; and *coffin* sounds like *coughing.*

3. a. cough
    b. course
    c. asked if she had been sick
    d. Sick people frequently cough, which sounds like course, and of course means "as you would expect" or "naturally."

Activity 7

1. a. pull, tooth
    b. tell, truth
    c. *judge* and *dentist*
    d. Judges are in court, where witnesses are sworn to "tell the truth, the whole truth, and nothing but the truth," and *truth* sounds like *tooth,* which is what a dentist sometimes pulls.

2. a. flight
    b. sight
    c. *attendant* and *met the pilot*
    d. Attendants and pilots both work on airplane flights, and "love at first flight" sounds like the familiar expression "love at first sight."

3. a. Flatman and Ribbon
    b. Batman and Robin
    c. *stampeding elephants*
    d. Anything in the path of stampeding elephants would be flattened (like a ribbon).

Activity 6

1. a. buoys
    b. boys
    c. *seagulls* and *hang out*
    d. Gulls and buoys are found at the sea; girls and boys hang out together; *gulls* sounds like *girls;* and *buoys* sounds like *boys.*

2. a. atomic
    b. a stomach
    c. *nuclear scientist* and *swallowed a uranium pill*
    d. Nuclear scientists study atomic reactions fueled by uranium, and swallowing a uranium pill would give you a stomachache.

3. a. eggs
    b. X
    c. *pirate, chicken, buried,* and *treasure*
    d. Pirates are associated with buried treasure, and chickens lay eggs, which sounds like X, as in the expression "X marks the spot."

Activity 8

1. a. Serious
    b. Series
    c. *baseball championship* and *not a laughing matter*
    d. The World Series is played to determine the baseball championship; and if something is serious, it should not cause laughter.

2. a. squeak
    b. speak
    c. *mouse*
    d. Mice squeak, and *squeak* sounds like *speak.*

3. a. ultraviolent
    b. ultraviolet
    c. *dangerous* and *light*
    d. Violent behavior is dangerous, *ultra* means "the most," and ultraviolet is a type of light.

UNIT 5: CHALLENGE ACTIVITIES

Activity 9

1.
   a. squeakers
   b. sneakers
   c. *mice* and *gym days*
   d. Mice squeak, *squeak* sounds like *sneak,* and sneakers are worn in a gym.

2.
   a. demons, ghoul's
   b. diamonds, girl's
   c. *demons, ghouls,* and *get along*
   d. "demons are a ghoul's best friend" sound like the song title "Diamonds Are a Girl's Best Friend."

3.
   a. peanutcillin
   b. penicillin
   c. *medicine, sick,* and *elephant*
   d. Elephants like to eat peanuts, and *peanutcillin* sounds like the medicine *penicillin.*

Activity 10

1.
   a. Panda
   b. Pan
   c. *bear* and *never grew up*
   d. A panda is thought of as a kind of bear, and *Peter Pan* is the story of a little boy who never wanted to grow up.

2.
   a. warts
   b. wars
   c. *galaxy* and *toad*
   d. The science fiction movie *Star Wars* takes place in a galaxy far, far away; toads are alleged to cause warts; and *Star Warts* sounds like *Star Wars.*

3.
   a. scar
   b. cigar
   c. *appendix removed* and *smoke*
   d. Removing one's appendix leaves a scar, and *scar* sounds like *cigar,* which is smoked especially during times of celebration, such as a successful operation.

Activity 11

1.
   a. fangfurters
   b. frankfurters
   c. Count Dracula and snack
   d. Dracula has fangs, and a frankfurter may be eaten as a snack.

2.
   a. dents
   b. dance
   c. auto mechanic
   d. Dents in cars are repaired at auto shops, and "Save the Last Dance for Me" is the title of a popular song.

3.
   a. Haunt
   b. Hut
   c. *ghosts* and *lunch*
   d. Ghosts haunt people, and Pizza Hut is a place to eat lunch.

UNIT 6: ADDITIONAL ACTIVITIES

Take Away One or More Sounds
at, latter, pat, patter, platter, sat, spat, splat
strain, train, stray, tray, rain, range, sane, say, ray
spin, in, it, print, pin, pit, spit, sin, sit

Take Away a Sound, Then Two: Activity 1
1. a. lash
   b. ash

2. a. talk
   b. auk

3. a. park
   b. par

4. a. trip
   b. rip

Take Away a Sound, Then Two: Activity 2
1. a. raid
   b. aid

2. a. troll
   b. roll

3. a. race
   b. ace

4. a. wore
   b. ore

Change a Sound
ball, well, call, fall, mall, tall, hall, will, Paul, Saul, wail, while, wool, walk
slit, slim, slick, sleep, slap, slope, clip, snip, blip, flip, slid
glass, crass, grease, gram, graph, gross, brass, grace, grab

Change a Sound, Then Two: Activity 1
1. a. glass
   b. glad

2. a. grow
   b. glow

3. a. stump
   b. slump

4. a. cluck
   b. stick

Change a Sound, Then Two: Activity 2
1. a. clap
   b. glum

2. a. string
   b. sprout

3. a. champ
   b. lamp

4. a. scheme
   b. step

UNIT 6: ADDITIONAL ACTIVITIES

Add a Sound

bead, beef, beak, beam, bean, beep, bees, beet, beat
bore, core, door, for, gore, lore, more, nor, poor, roar, sore, soar, tore, wore
bin, din, fin, kin, pin, sin, tin, thin, win

Add a Sound, Then Two: Activity 1

1. a. lend
   b. blend

2. a. link
   b. blink

3. a. land
   b. bland

4. a. lever
   b. clever

Add a Sound, Then Two: Activity 2

1. a. lace
   b. place

2. a. pin
   b. spin

3. a. late
   b. plate

4. a. tend
   b. trend

Take Away, Change, and Add a Sound

1. lea, lake, sleek
2. pay, pray, played
3. feet, fast, feasts
4. ail, pale, frail
5. ray, tree, stray
6. tip, trick, strip
7. odd, cod, prod
8. ear, fear, tears; air, pair, stare
9. ill, sell, still
10. and, bind, brand
11. sick, stock, sticky
12. may, make, maimed
13. mile, mails, smiles
14. row, crow, grown
15. reek, crack, creeks

Words with One or Two Sounds

Peter Pan

1. Peter Panda
2. Peter Pants
3. Peter Pans
4. Peter Panics
5. Peter Panther

The Princess and the Pea

1. The Princess and the Peel
2. The Princess and the Peak
3. The Princess and the Peach
4. The Princess and the Peep
5. The Princess and the Peace

UNIT 6: ADDITIONAL ACTIVITIES

Words with Three Sounds
1. pat, pet, pit, pot, put, putt, peat
2. sad, sod, side, sued, seed, sewed, sighed
3. ran, rag, rub, run, race, rose, rail, wrote, road, rack, ram, rap, raise
4. van, vine, vain, veil, vase, vote, vogue, vague, vat, veal, vile, vibe
5. beak, back, cake, sick, wake, walk, make, neck, talk, buck, rack, knock
6. him, ham, hem, dim, rim, comb, came, lamb, time, lame, room
7. leg, log, lag, lot, lake, lane, line, loot, loom, lose, loose, laugh
8. leaf, loaf, beef, safe, muff, miff, cough, laugh
9. wall, well, wet, will, wile, wick, wait, wade, wane, weight
10. lag, leg, beg, big, bug, bag, fog, gig, fig, shag, chug

Words with Four Sounds
1. clan, clone, clown, clean, crown, crane
2. stun, stone, stain, slain, Spain, spine
3. lamp, last, left, least, loafed, laughed
4. rest, romp, rails, roast, raced, river
5. stop, sleep, clap, drop, grape, elope
6. bleak, black, click, crack, snake, steak
7. step, stop, stove, stall, stick, stock, steep, stale
8. prom, prim, prune, prize, prone, prose, prawn, proud
9. slot, slip, slim, slap, sleep, slide, slime, slope, slate
10. trap, trip, trod, trim, tread, treat, trade, trees, trick

---

Knock-Knock Jokes: Activity 1
1. Jimmy, gimme
2. Izzy, easy
3. Jaws, yours
4. Kent, can't

Knock-Knock Jokes: Activity 2
1. Leif, leave
2. Nettie, nutty
3. Shirley, surely
4. Vaughn, one

Knock-Knock Jokes: Activity 3
1. voodoo, who do
2. whittle, little
3. yelp, help
4. yachts, what's

Knock-Knock Jokes: Activity 4
1. safe, save
2. Sid, sit
3. free, three
4. Zeke, seek

Knock-Knock Jokes: Activity 5
1. pet, put
2. Salon, so long
3. Fannybody, anybody
4. Freddie, ready

Knock-Knock Jokes: Activity 6
1. Harry, hurry
2. myth, miss
3. scissor, Caesar
4. Barton, button

Knock-Knock Jokes: Activity 7
1. Dwayne, dwouning, drain, drowning
2. Luke, look
3. Don, don't
4. ears, here's

Knock-Knock Jokes: Activity 8
1. Tars and Tripes, Stars and Stripes
2. Sarah, is there a
3. Noman, no man
4. Gladys, glad it's

APPENDIX

CONSONANT SOUNDS

/b/ as in **b**oy

/d/ as in **d**og

/f/ as in **f**ig, lau**gh**, **ph**one

/g/ as in **g**oat, va**gue**

/h/ as in **h**at, **wh**ose

/ʤ/ as in e**d**ucate, we**dge**, **g**iant, exa**gg**erate, **j**oke

/k/ as in **c**ar, o**cc**asion, **ch**rome, du**ck**, **k**ite, **q**uick, pi**que**

/l/ as in **l**ove, bi**ll**

/m/ as in **m**oney, co**mb**, dru**mm**er, hy**mn**

/n/ as in **gn**at, **kn**ee, **n**ight, su**nn**y, **pn**eumonia

/ŋ/ as in si**ng**

/p/ as in **p**at, a**pp**ear

/r/ as in **r**ain, ca**rr**ot

/s/ as in **c**ity, **s**it, exce**ss**

/ʃ/ as in a**ss**ociate, **ch**ampagne, musi**ci**an, **s**ure, **sh**eep, dimen**si**on, pre**ss**ure, na**ti**on

/t/ as in **t**op, mu**tt**

/ʧ/ as in **ch**alk, **c**ello, **c**ultural, celes**ti**al

/θ/ as in **th**ick (voiceless)

/ð/ as in **th**ose (voiced)

/v/ as in **v**ine

/w/ as in **o**ne, jag**u**ar, **w**ater, **wh**ite

/j/ as in **E**ugene, torti**ll**a, **u**se, **y**ellow

/z/ as in **cz**ar, hi**s**, **X**erox, **z**ipper, bu**zz**

/ʒ/ as in re**g**ime, rou**ge**, bi**j**ou, trea**s**ure, A**si**a, a**z**ure

VOWEL SOUNDS

/i/ as in al*gae*, b*e*, s*ee*, fl*ea*, k*ey*, sk*i*, sweet*ie*, Hawa*ii*, debr*is*, espr*it*, grand pr*ix*, fan*cy*

/ɪ/ as in *it*, w*o*men, rh*y*thm

/eɪ/ as in *maple*, parf*ait*, w*ay*, per s*e*, caf*é*, w*eigh*, f*oy*er, h*ey*

/ɛ/ as in b*et*, d*ea*f

/æ/ as in *at*, pl*ai*d

/u/ as in st*ew*, l*ieu*, v*iew*, S*ioux*, d*o*, sh*oe*, t*oo*, y*ou*, thr*ough*, fl*u*, d*ue*, H*ugh*, s*ui*t, deb*ut*, tw*o*

/ʊ/ as in c*oo*k, w*ou*ld

/oʊ/ as in f*aux*, b*eau*, g*o*, wh*oa*, f*oe*, *oh*, d*ough*, l*ow*

/ɔ/ as in *all* c*augh*t, r*aw*, *off*

/ɑ/ as in h*a*, bl*ah*, f*aux* pas, h*o*t

/ʌ/ (stressed) as in am*o*k, fl*oo*d, c*u*t, d*uh*

/ɝ/ (stressed) as in h*er*, w*ere*, f*ir*, bl*ur*, s*ure*, p*urr*, m*yrrh*

/ə/ (unstressed) as in cap*a*ble, op*e*n, reproduc*i*ble, t*o*day, moonstr*u*ck

/ɚ/ (unstressed) as in li*ar*, bett*er*, amat*eur*, sweatsh*ir*t, profess*or*, theat*re*, conc*ur*, cens*ure*, mart*yr*

/ɑɪ/ as in samur*ai*, *aye*, h*ei*ght, *eye*, h*i*, l*ie*, s*igh*, b*uy*, m*y*, r*ye*

/ɔɪ/ as in *oil*, Illin*oi*s, t*oy*

/ɑʊ/ as in *out*, b*ough*, h*ow*

IDIOM AND PROVERB DICTIONARIES

Chapman, R.L. (Ed.). (1986). *New dictionary of American slang*. New York: Harper & Row.

Gulland, D.M., & Hinds-Howell, D.G. (1994). *Dictionary of English idioms*. New York: Penguin Books.

Makkai, A., Boatner, M.T., & Gates, J.E. (1995). *A dictionary of American idioms*. New York: Barron's Educational Series.

Simpson, J. (1996). *The concise Oxford dictionary of proverbs*. New York: Oxford University Press.

Spears, R.A. (1994). *Essential American idioms*. Lincolnwood, IL: National Textbook Co.

Spears, R.A. (1996). *NTC's American idioms dictionary*. Lincolnwood, IL: National Textbook Co.

REFERENCES

Adams, M.J. (1990). *Beginning to read: Thinking and learning about print*. Cambridge, MA: MIT Press.

Apthorp, H. (1995). Phonetic coding and reading in college students with and without learning disability. *Journal of Learning Disability, 28*(6), 342–352.

Ball, E.W. (1997). Phonological awareness: Implica-tions for whole language and emergent literacy programs. *Topics in Language Disorders, 17*(3), 14–26.

Ball, E.W., & Blachman, B.A. (1988). Phoneme segmentation training: Effect on reading readiness. *Annals of Dyslexia, 38*, 208–225.

Ball, E.W., & Blachman, B.A. (1991). Does phoneme awareness training in kindergarten make a difference in early word recognition and developmental spelling? *Reading Research Quarterly, 26*, 49–66.

Bird, J., Bishop, D.V.M., & Freeman, N.H. (1995). Phonological awareness and literacy development in children with expressive phonological impairments. *Journal of Speech and Hearing Research, 38*, 446–462.

Blachman, B.A. (1991). Early intervention for children's reading problems: Clinical applications of the research in phonological awareness. *Topics in Language Disorders, 12*(1), 51–65.

Blachman, B.A. (1994). Early literacy acquisition: The role of phonological awareness. In G.P. Wallach & K.G. Butler (Eds.), *Language learning disabilities in school-age children and adolescents: Some principles and applications* (pp. 253–274). New York: Macmillan.

Bradley, L., & Bryant, P. (1983). Categorizing sounds and learning to read: A causal connection. *Nature, 30*, 419–421.

Bradley, L., & Bryant, P. (1985). *Rhyme and reason in reading and spelling*. Ann Arbor, MI: University of Michigan Press.

Bradley, L., & Bryant, P. (1991). Phonological skills before and after learning to read. In S.A. Brady & D.P. Shankweiler (Eds.), *Phonological processes in literacy: A tribute to Isabelle Y. Liberman* (pp. 37–45). Hillsdale, NJ: Lawrence Erlbaum Associates.

Browder, D. (2008). Rethinking literacy expectations for students with significant disabilities. Retrieved on March 3, 2008, from http://www.speechpathology.com/interview_detail.asp?interview_id=1120

Catts, H.W. (1993). The relationship between speech-language impairments and reading disabilities. *Journal of Speech and Hearing Research, 36*, 948–958.

Clarke-Klein, S.M. (1994). Expressive phonological deficiencies: Impact on spelling development. *Topics in Language Disorders, 14*(2), 40–55.

Donahue, M., & Bryan, T. (1984). Communicative skills and peer relations of learning disabled adolescents. *Topics in Language Disorders, 4*(2), 10–21.

Fischer, F.W., Shankweiler, D., & Liberman, I. (1985). Spelling proficiency and sensitivity to word structure. *Journal of Memory and Language, 24*, 423–441.

Fletcher, J.M., Shaywitz, S.E., Shankweiler, D.P., Katz, L., Liberman, I.Y., Stuebing, K., et al. (1994). Cognitive profiles of reading disability: Comparisons of discrepancy and low achievement definitions. *Journal of Educational Psychology, 86*(1), 6–23.

Gillon, G., & Dodd, B. (1995). The effects of training phonological, semantic, and syntactic processing skills in spoken language on reading ability. *Language, Speech, and Hearing Services in Schools, 26*, 58–68.

Gillon, G.T. (2002, December). Phonological awareness intervention for children: From the research laboratory to the clinic. *ASHA Leader*.

Gough, P.B., Juel, C., & Griffith, P.L. (1992). Reading, spelling, and the orthographic cluster. In P.B. Gough, L.C. Ehri, & R.A. Treiman (Eds.), *Reading acquisition* (pp. 35–48). Hillsdale, NJ: Lawrence Erlbaum Associates.

Green, T.A., & Pepicello, W.J. (1978). Wit in riddling: A linguistic perspective. *Genre, 11*, 1–13.

Hodson, B.W. (1994). Helping individuals become intelligible, literate, and articulate: The role of phonology. *Topics in Language Disorders, 14*(2), 1–16.

Hogan, T.P., Catts, H.W., & Little, T.D. (2005). The relationship between phonological awareness and reading. *Language, Speech, and Hearing Services in Schools, 36*, 285–293.

Hurford, D.P., Johnston, M., Nepote, P., Hampton, S., Moore, S., Neal, J., et al. (1994). Early identification and remediation of phonological processing deficits in first-grade children at risk for reading disabilities. *Journal of Learning Disability, 27*(10), 647–659.

Kitz, W., & Tarver, S. (1989). Comparison of dyslexic and nondyslexic adults on decoding and phonemic awareness tasks. *Annals of Dyslexia, 39*, 196–205.

Liberman, I.Y., Shankweiler, D., & Liberman, A.M. (1989). The alphabetic principle and learning to read. In D. Shankweiler & I.Y. Liberman (Eds.), *Phonology and reading disability: Solving the reading puzzle* (IARLD Monograph Series). Ann Arbor, MI: University of Michigan Press.

Lindamood, C.H., & Lindamood, P.C. (1979). *Lindamood auditory conceptualization test*. Allen, TX: DLM Teaching Resources.

Lundberg, I., Frost, J., & Petersen, O. (1988). Effects of an extensive program for stimulating phonological awareness in preschool children. *Reading Research Quarterly, 23*, 263–284.

MacDonald, G.W., & Cornwall, A. (1995). The relationship between phonological awareness and reading and spelling achievement eleven years later. *Journal of Learning Disability, 28*(8), 523–527.

McGregor, K.K. (1994). Use of phonological information in a word-finding treatment for children. *Journal of Speech and Hearing Research, 37,* 1381–1393.

Menyuk, P., & Chesnick, M. (1997). Metalinguistic skills, oral language knowledge, and reading. *Topics in Language Disorders, 17*(3), 75–87.

Morais, J. (1991). Phonological awareness: A bridge between language and literacy. In D. Sawyer & B. Fox (Eds.), *Phonological awareness in reading.* New York: Springer-Verlag.

Nippold, M.A. (1988). Linguistic ambiguity. In M.A. Nippold (Ed.), *Later language development: Ages nine through nineteen* (pp. 211–223). Boston: College-Hill.

Pennington, B.F., Van Orden, G.C., Smith, S.D., Green, P.A., & Haith, M.M. (1990). Phonological processing skills and deficits in adult dyslexics. *Child Development, 61,* 1753–1778.

Pepicello, W.J. (1980). Linguistic strategies in riddling. *Western Folklore, 39,* 1–16.

Perfetti, C.A. (1991). Representations and awareness in the acquisition of reading competence. In L. Rieben & C.A. Perfetti (Eds.), *Learning to read: Basic research and its implications* (pp. 33–46). Hillsdale, NJ: Lawrence Erlbaum Associates.

Pokorni, J., Worthington, C., & Jamison, P. (2004). Phonological awareness intervention: Comparison of Fast ForWord, Earobics, and LiPS. *Journal of Educational Research, 97,* 147–157.

Pressley, M., & Rankin, J. (1994). More about whole language methods of reading instruction for students at risk for early school failure. *Learning Disabilities Research and Practice, 9*(3), 157–168.

Robertson, C., & Salter, W. (2007). *The phonological awareness test 2.* East Moline, IL: LinguiSystems.

Robertson, K. (1993). *Phonological awareness in kindergarten children of differing socio-economic status.* Master's thesis. University of Rhode Island, Kingston.

Rubba, J. (2004). Phonological awareness skills and spelling skills. Retrieved February 19, 2008, from http://cla.calpoly.edu/-jrubba/phon/phonaware.html

Schuele, M.C., & Boudreau, D. (2008). Phonological awareness intervention: Beyond the basics. *Language, Speech, and Hearing Services in Schools, 39,* 3–20.

Snyder, L.S., & Downey, D. (1991). The language–reading relationship in normal and reading disabled children. *Journal of Speech and Hearing Research, 34,* 129–140.

Spector, C.C. (1990). Linguistic humor comprehension of normal and language-impaired adolescents. *Journal of Speech and Hearing Disorders, 55,* 533–541.

Spector, C.C. (1992). Remediating humor comprehension deficits in language-impaired students. *Language, Speech, and Hearing Services in Schools, 23,* 20–27.

Spector, C.C. (1997, November). *Children's comprehension of linguistic humor based on phoneme level changes.* Poster session presented at the annual convention of the American Speech-Language-Hearing Association, Boston.

Stackhouse, J. (1997). Phonological awareness: Connecting speech and literacy problems. In B.W. Hodson & M.L. Edwards (Eds.), *Perspectives in applied phonology* (pp. 157–196). Gaithersburg, MD: Aspen.

Stothard, S.C., Snowling, M.J., Bishop, D.V.M., Chipchase, B.B., & Kaplan, C.A. (1998). Language-impaired preschoolers: A follow-up into adolescence. *Journal of Speech, Language, and Hearing Research, 41,* 407–418.

Surdak-Upright, L. (1998, April). *Phonemic awareness: Beyond theory.* Seminar presented at the annual convention of the New York State Speech-Language-Hearing Association.

Swanson, T.J., Hodson, B.W., & Schommer-Aikins, M. (2005). An examination of phonological awareness treatment outcomes for seventh-grade poor readers from a bilingual community. *Language, Speech, and Hearing Services in Schools, 36,* 336–345.

Torgesen, J.K., & Bryant, B.R. (2004). *Test of phonological awareness–second edition: PLUS.* East Moline, IL: LinguiSystems.

Torgesen, J.K., Wagner, R.K., & Rashotte, C. (1994). Longitudinal studies of phonological processing and reading. *Journal of Learning Disability, 27,* 276–286.

Treiman, R. (1991). Phonological awareness and its roles in learning to read and spell. In D. Sawyer & B. Fox (Eds.), *Phonological awareness in reading.* New York: Springer-Verlag.

Ukrainetz, T. (2006). Scaffolding young students into phonemic awareness. In T. Ukrainetz (Ed.), *Contextualized language intervention: Scaffolding PreK–12 literacy achievement* (pp. 429–467). Eau Claire, WI: Thinking Publications.

van Kleeck, A. (1990). Emergent literacy: Learning about print before learning to read. *Topics in Language Disorders, 10*(2), 25–45.

Wagner, R., & Torgesen, J. (1987). The nature of phonological processing and its causal role in the acquisition of reading skills. *Psychological Bulletin, 101,* 192–212.

Wagner, R., Torgesen, J., & Rashotte, C. (1999). *Comprehensive test of phonological processing.* Austin, TX: Pro-Ed.

Wallach, G.P., & Miller, L. (1988). *Language intervention and academic success.* Boston: College-Hill Press.

Wiig, E.H. (1984). Language disabilities in adolescents: A question of cognitive strategies. *Topics in Language Disorders, 4*(2), 41–58.

Williams, J. (1986). The role of phonemic analysis in reading. In J. Torgesen & B. Wong (Eds.), *Psychological and educational perspectives on learning disabilities* (pp. 399–416). Orlando, FL: Academic Press.